MINI 50 YEARS

ROB GOLDING

MOTORBOOKS

First published in 2007 by Motorbooks, an imprint of MBI Publishing Company LLC, Galtier Plaza, Suite 200, 380 Jackson Street, St. Paul, MN 55101-3885 USA

Motorbooks titles are also available at discounts in bulk quantity for industrial or sales-promotional use. For details write to Special Sales Manager at MBI Publishing Company, Galtier Plaza, Suite 200, 380 Jackson Street, St. Paul, MN 55101-3885 USA.

To find out more about our books, join us online at www.motorbooks.com.

ISBN-13: 978-0-7603-2627-5
ISBN-10: 0-7603-2627-4

Editor: Lindsay Hitch
Designer: Sara Holle

Printed in China

Library of Congress Cataloging-in-Publication Data

Golding, Rob, 1950-
  Mini 50 years / Rob Golding.
      p. cm.
  Includes index.
  ISBN-13: 978-0-7603-2627-5 (plc)
  ISBN-10: 0-7603-2627-4 (plc)
  1. Mini automobiles—History. I. Title.
TL215.M465G65 2007
629.222'2—dc22

                            2006035319

About the Author: Rob Golding has become the recognized Mini biographer, having written *Mini*, *Mini After 25 Years*, *Mini: Thirty Years On*, and *Mini: Thirty-Five Years On*. He has tracked the car's fifty years of development while working as a motoring and motorsports writer, as a business journalist, and as an auto industry analyst. For his latest book on the subject, he was given unrivaled access to the people who made the story.

Note: Currency values in this book are translated out of pounds sterling at Q3 2006 rates. They are not adjusted for differing rates of translation over time and do not allow for different prices in different markets.

On the cover: Mini Cooper S. *David Newhardt*

On the title page: Mini Knightsbridge: One of four final edition models for classic Mini.

On the back cover:
Mini Cooper S: One of four final edition models for classic Mini.

In MISSION MINI in 2002, 21 international teams brought to life Val McDermid's unfinished crime novel to rescue the stolen paintings of New York artist Peter Halley. After 36 hours, the German team successfully located the artwork.

The new MINI Cooper S and MINI Cooper launched November 18, 2006.

Contents

Acknowledgments

BMW has been very gentle with the MINI history. Its people have teased the essence out of the legend and caused little offence to those who remember well the liberating and stimulating nature of cheap and quick transport in the 1960s. Mini was special because it was a rebel. It was able to stuff Jaguars on the country lanes on the way to the pub, and it was able to humiliate massive, growling Ford Falcons on the racetracks. Middle-aged men would not have taken kindly to quality nostalgia being obscured by a bunch of profit-hungry German businessmen.

The enduring impression of the people who have wrung a fantastically successful business out of the industrial boneyard of original Mini is that they care about the heritage in a major way. They realise that guys like Issigonis do not come along that often and when they do they are rarely given carte blanche to force through a radical proposal. The wrong thing would have been to apply modern thought to new MINI without regard for what the inventor might have thought. The right response was to carry original concept very much top of mind. That is what was done. "Safe in their hands" is one way of expressing it. I prefer to think that there is rather more energy than that, and that the road ahead will be characterised more by excitement than by safety.

There is not too much about Issigonis in this book in contrast to my previous book, *MINI 35 Years On*, now out of print. Keen students of the old boy—who would have been 100, had he lived, on the day that second-generation MINI went on sale—could do worse than look at *Alec Issigonis, the Man who made the Mini* by Jonathan Wood. Another chum who added to the sum of knowledge was Andrew Lorenz, who co-authored *End of the Road: BMW and Rover— a brand too far*.

The task of this book has been to weld up all the events that brought us to this point, starting with the instruction to Issigonis in 1956 to design a small car that would allow the British Motor Corporation to clean up in a market worried by the Suez crisis.

Many of my interviewees on the early history are now gone, including Sir Alec himself, of course, and John Cooper. Had I not interviewed those two legends at length in 1978 and 1979 for *Mini*—the first book in this series— my interest might not have lasted this long.

My thanks to Tim Parker, who commissioned all my MINI books, and to Chris Willows. who runs public affairs at BMW in the UK. Chris understands the value of books and is able to overlook the distraction caused to the organisation by the people who research and write them. His colleagues Mark Harrison and Ellysia Graymore generated all the access that was necessary in several countries. Ellysia was

key. She bore the brunt of all the outrageous demands and transacted them with everlasting energy and humour.

Many people are quoted in the book and of course each and every one of those people has been a material help. But I must make special mention of Paul Chantry, Kay Segler, Gert Hildebrand, Mike Cooper (who added to all the wisdom gathered from his father, John Cooper, before his death), Paddy Hopkirk, Harald Krüger, Marc Eden, Frank Stephenson, Bernd Pischetsrieder, Paul Mullett, Helen Webster, Gabe Bridger, and Russ Swift.

Introduction
Mini Trinity
Classic, Current, and Future

In the beginning, there was Sir Alec Issigonis, a man as mean as chicken broth but with the air of a wealthy English aristocrat. He made the Mini because he was absorbed by minimalism. Its delivery suited the era. The challenge of creating it suited the man.

Successive attempts were made to change the classic Mini during its 41 years in production. That was a tough task. The few changes that were introduced—such as the Clubman front end and Wolseley and Riley brands—were reversed before the end of the Mini's life.

Sir Alec Issigonis did not have formal engineering training. He mockingly described himself as an ironmonger. Others saw him as a cranky inventor, but he was a great visualiser, and all those who worked with him were well used to getting memos in the form of da Vinci–esque drawings—often doodled on restaurant tablecloths. These little sketches explained how a four-seater car could be reduced to an overall length of just 10 feet, how front-wheel drive would work, and how an engine could be mounted transversely in the front.

So obsessive was his determination to retain the minimum space, weight, and dimension that Issigonis omitted some of the obvious requirements. Seat belt mounting points, for example, were initially missing because he did not use seat belts himself. There was nowhere for a radio because he thought it a distraction while driving.

Because the Mini's wheels were pushed away to the corners of the car to avoid intrusion on the passenger space, the car derived the benefit of extraordinary stability, which endowed it with tenacious road holding. That in turn generated a tuning industry that bumped Mini's performance up to match handling, and that spawned race and rally programmes that blew away the performance cars of the era.

The endearing looks and scurry-hurry demeanour of the car on the road generated an affection that crossed social divides. Car ownership, generally, grew at a frantic pace during Mini's early life and outgrew on-street parking provisions in London. The Mini's overall length meant that its driver could always grab the last parking space available. That had such value to the trendy young men about town

Sir Alec Issigonis with Lord Snowdon, who married the Queen's sister Margaret, and was an early smart-set Mini adopter.

that they would gladly give up the Jaguar to gain the convenience of being able to park. More than 5 million classic Minis were built in its lifetime, 318,000 a year at the peak.

Then came BMW. The German company bought MG Rover in 1994, by which time Mini production was down to a trickle of 20,000 a year. The BMW group knew that Mini was a brand that might help it spread activities down the size and price range to complete its market coverage from entry level to limousine. Rolls-Royce was bought to cover the premium end in 1998. But BMW had more urgent tasks to confront in 1994 than replacement of Mini. The effort and investment went first into mainstream models such as the Rover 75.

During the four-year period between 1994 and 1998, a power battle raged between BMW and MG Rover engineers as to what the new MINI should be like. The BMW hierarchy was itself keen that there should be some creative tension—the BMW engineers were the world's best in execution, but the UK was the spiritual and emotional home of the brand and had more intuitive feel for the product. For most of that time, many imagined that there would be revolutionary rather than evolutionary design and that the new MINI would be a modern take on efficient packaging in the

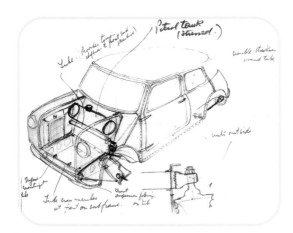

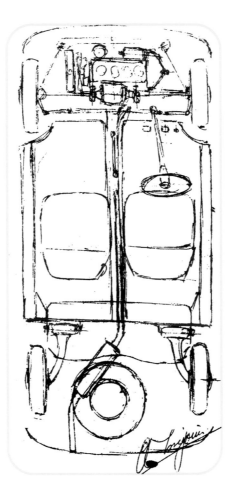

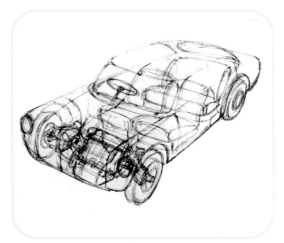

These three drawings by Issigonis illustrate his simple style, which is both imaginative and entertaining.

way that the original had been. The early concepts that came up for review were in the mould of the Mercedes A-class (being readied for introduction in 1998). MINI was to become tall and thin and a one-box configuration. The German designers, though, had a belief that the Mini brand and its distinctive appearance were of huge value and in no way should the combination be broken up.

The leading light in the debate was BMW designer Frank Stephenson, and he went back to his home in Munich one night and cast himself in the role of Issigonis. On a length of kitchen towel, he sketched a 1969 update as it might have been had the original Mini been updated in line with contemporary trends and available technology. Then he did the same for a 1979 update . . . and then a 1989 new model launch. From that process came his "1999 MINI." The selected design was finally taking shape. New MINI was quite a bit bigger than the original, but it was unmistakably an evolution. The key features preserved were the upright wheelhouse and the separate bonnet—despite its negative effect on aerodynamic efficiency. Once the view was taken that fuel economy would be uncompetitive relative to other small cars, the stage was set for an emphasis on performance, and that meant positioning at a premium price within the small-car class.

Even today, the leading minds at MINI HQ in Munich still cast themselves in the mould of Issigonis. It is regarded as an essential discipline to maintain the essence of the brand: "Be true to what you believe," was one quote.

"Issigonis was arrogant and therefore so am I," was another. It is a very strict "we do things differently" approach, and it infects every part of the organisation in its ceaseless aspiration to stand apart from a me-too small-car market. Even when planning the press launch, the start point was "how does everyone else do it? So we don't do it like that, then."

Now Here Comes the New Generation

The graduation to 2007 MINI was a curious affair. Speculation was stoked to a frenzy on specialist web-sites—the American site, MotoringFile.com, and MINI2.com in the UK in particular—as to how the phenomenally successful car could be improved. The debate was fed by testing shots and inspired nuggets of contributed information that could not possibly have been leaked from the MINI inner sanctum.

One thing that was particularly curious was that the makeover was to be only five-and-a-bit years after the launch of the original, rather than the more common eight. The reasoning was simple: the current car was not capable of passing imminent pedestrian crash safety regulations, and structural changes would be needed anyway. As new derivatives, led by the Traveller, were coming down the chute, the decision was made to change the basic platform early. Expansion of the factory at Oxford was vital to raise production and meet demand, and the new car could best be introduced simultaneous with the new capacity.

In 1960s saloon car racing championships, the Mini was always the one hiding in the blue tyre smoke.

The crash test change triggered a huge number of contingent design changes. When a car hits a pedestrian on the lower leg, he is flung onto the bonnet rather than knocked flat. His head hits the bonnet, and there has to be sufficient crumple space between the bonnet and the engine block to cushion the impact. A bonnet height change (2 centimetres taller at the trailing edge) forced a higher waistline for the new MINI and created a shallower glasshouse to preserve the same overall height. The changes to the body thereafter are almost indistinguishable to a casual observer, but they are numerous.

Timo Makinen with Tony Fall in the hot seat running in the 1967 RAC Rally.

From the front, the clue is the headlamp treatment. Instead of being mounted in the bonnet, the lamps are fixed to the body and show through cutouts. The wheel arch protectors have also moved from the clamshell bonnet

The inspiration behind MINI style was Frank Stephenson, who penned the sketches that convinced BMW to take the derivative route.

Below: One of the Stephenson sketches that gave BMW the confidence to recreate MINI.

In the original, the headlamps went up with the bonnet and constantly needed realignment. The second-generation car has the lights anchored to the body with cutouts in the bonnet.

The new BMW 1,600cc Cooper S Turbo engine in cutaway form.

panel to the side frame to save nudge damage to that complex bonnet pressing.

From the back, there is a subtle change to the glass-to-metal joint on the C-pillar. From the side, only the most perceptive eye can see that the car is the same height, but 2 centimetres taller at the waistline. There is a more muscular curve to the side panel and boot panel. That improves boot space a tad and extends overall length by 6 centimetres. The result is that every body panel is new—even the (stiffer) roof.

The other design priority was to improve fuel consumption and emissions. That also created many knock-on effects.

The new platform has a full underbody shield to regain some airflow efficiency. Out goes the unburstable Chrysler Tritec engine made in Brazil, and in comes a more efficient petrol unit designed by BMW and developed jointly with PSA. It is made in France, but the BMW version is assembled at Hams Hall near Birmingham. PSA also hoped to become the provider of a diesel in place of Toyota, which had the only offering that fitted the 2001 MINI engine bay.

The steering is electric-assist, and the transmission changes from CVT to six-speed auto on all models (the same basic design as the Golf GTI box). The loss of the CVT

Style across the years—the Frank Stephenson sketch in 1998 was the inspiration for current MINI. The second-generation sketch clearly shows how little change was required.

transmission whine, together with the change from super-charger to turbo (on the Cooper S), changes the drive-by note. Both of these changes improve fuel economy. The latest MINI has a new interior, new handling characteristics, new steering, and new drive-by sound.

Preferences were added to the design brief to get a slightly more sophisticated ride and reduce cabin noise. This was deemed of particular importance to the U.S. market, where there is little familiarity with deliberately sporty

While the exterior of BMW's second-generation MINI is barely changed, the funky interior style has been enhanced and upgraded substantially.

ride, handling, and engine noise. However, the distinctive go-kart feel, tenacious grip, and throttle steer have been maintained or improved. More space was created in the footwells—both width and depth. There are financial benefits for BMW in the changes. The car is easier to assemble than before and is therefore cheaper. The whole of the front-end assembly is outsourced and delivered lineside. The shared 1,600cc engine will have production volumes of 1 million and scale benefit.

It has been a gamble—of that there is no doubt. The designers and engineers still wonder whether they were clever in managing to change the exterior of the car completely without any perceived change of appearance—or whether this would have been the moment to move the styling on a generation.

Only time will tell. But the comforting factor for BMW is that there will now be a steady trickle of derivatives—starting with the concept referred to as Traveller, but unlikely to be called that.

Chapter 1

Issigonis Starts Work

Right: Issigonis was responsible for the Morris Minor before the Mini.

Fifty years ago, in September 1956, Gamal Abdel Nasser of Egypt created the Suez Crisis and, unintentionally, the Mini.

The president nationalised the Suez Canal, which was then the world's most important transport passageway, as it allowed tanker vessels to go the short way around Africa and to much reduce the time and cost involved in shipping oil from the wells of the Middle East. The French and British who built and owned the canal and enjoyed charging tolls were displeased. The Americans who used a lot of oil were equally displeased, and the Jewish lobby was startled at the sudden threat to peace in the region so soon after World War II settlements.

At Longbridge in Birmingham, England, Leonard (later Sir Leonard) Lord had spent the previous several months trying to decide what type of new car was most urgent. The end of World War II 10 years earlier had suggested that the country was ready for an era of extravagance with large saloons and fancy sports cars. Yet postwar austerity persisted, and the economics were against large-scale success for such vehicles.

When the Suez Canal was cut, Lord dithered no longer. He sent for Issigonis, his head of design, who had recently returned from a four-year stint down the road at Alvis, and told him to drop everything and build something tiny. The crisis would affect oil prices, he reasoned, and the market requirement for years to come was going to be for frugal transport.

Before Issigonis had left to join Alvis—the weapons company that also had a lovely range of sports saloons—he had been experimenting with front-drive arrangements for the Morris Minor, a car that was also his design. When he got back to Longbridge in 1956, Issigonis found that his ideas had been progressed and had worked extremely well in experimental vehicles. Front drive had even been taken up the size range to the point that a prototype, which eventually became the Austin 1800, was also running happily.

No one is quite sure how the Mini name first arose (the style was always Mini under British ownership and MINI under BMW, which will be helpful in discriminating between the two generations of car), but the probable origins of it trace back to the initial briefing that Issigonis got from

A cutaway of the early classic Mini showing the compact arrangement.

Leonard Lord. He was told to produce a miniature of the Morris Minor that would use minimal materials surrounding the minimum space necessary to contain four people. An additional contributor to the thought process was the two-cylinder engine that was briefly tested in a prototype. To discriminate, it became known as the mini motor.

Issigonis' response to Lord's mandate was literal. He formed a team of eight people, then took four wooden canteen chairs and laid them out on the workshop floor in two rows of two, and sat half his team down. Then they shuffled the chairs around until a consensus emerged that the minimum space had been established, and the parameters were preserved with chalk marks on the workshop floor.

Sir Alec Issigonis stands with a car less to his liking—the Maxi.

Sir Alec with the very
first production car and
the little-changed
January 1965 update.

Sir Alec at Oulton Park in 1961 with his Lightweight Special.

Issigonis took out a tape measure and calculated that without allowing for boot or bonnet (trunk or hood), the car would need to be at least 8 feet 9 inches long, 4 feet 2 inches wide, and 4 feet 4 inches high.

It would be some time before the Morris Mini Minor name took hold within the company, because the code name of this project was Austin Newmarket. The parent company for the merged brands, the British Motor Corporation (BMC), was in the habit of giving its cars place names—Oxford, Cambridge, Westminster, and the like—and this tiny thing was to address an entirely new market, occupied hitherto only by vulnerable and risible bubble cars.

Issigonis had already decided that the Newmarket had to be front-wheel drive. During his time away at Alvis, the experimental workshops had been testing ever-larger cars with this arrangement, and Citroën had put it into production perfectly well in the Traction Avant (front drive). The big advantage was the space it saved in the cabin by removing the transmission tunnel needed for the prop shaft.

But because Issigonis envisaged a car that was low to the ground, he retained a vestigial tunnel to contain the exhaust system and ensured that the exhaust and the car had a 6-inch ground clearance. A transverse engine would save space. That also had already been proven elsewhere. The tricky bit was deciding what to do with the gearbox.

Issigonis was tempted to accommodate the gearbox in line with the cylinder block, but to do so within the width of 4 feet 2 inches he would have needed to make the trans-verse engine a two-cylinder rather than four—incompatible with the performance profiles that he had in mind. The only remaining unused space in the engine bay was below the engine. To place the gearbox there was unheard of, but no matter. Meeting and beating the challenge of innovation was a daily activity for the tall, lean Greek.

Just as well. Time was short. The travails of BMC were multiplying, and the grip that it had on world markets—established by right just after World War II—was sliding. Sir Leonard Lord wanted the Newmarket in production quickly. On the timetable that had been agreed upon with the development department, Issigonis had to freeze the design by July 1958. That meant that he had only six months to prove that the engine and gearbox could be combined and would run happily in shared sump oil. Clearly, the number of testing miles would be limited by the timetable. Issigonis simply decided that all would be okay and struck out into unexplored territory.

In July 1958, Issigonis took his running prototype to Leonard Lord. Lord drove it round the factory car park for five minutes, according to Issigonis. Without any apparent reservations, Lord asked for it to be in production within 12 months. It was, but the speed of process left the Mini with some problems.

The gearbox in the sump worked, but two other major technical obstacles had to be overcome to generate a functional, safe, and enjoyable consumer product. One was the driveshafts. Because this car would achieve high speeds on

This was the Longbridge engineering department buck that assessed the minimum cabin size required for four adults.

very small wheels, the shafts would have to rotate at high speed. In addition, to make the most of its compact dimensions, Mini needed great handling and manoeuvrability, which meant a great turning radius. There were no existing driveshafts that would do the job, and Issigonis had to go to a supplier of submarine conning tower control gear to find patents that allowed production of the kit that would do the job for him. In fact, Leonard Lord liked the constant velocity (CV) joint so much, he bought the company. It was then called Unipower and was based in Shipley in Yorkshire, England.

Hardy-Spicer, by then a GKN company, did the development work, and from that initial relationship sprang the largest CV joint supplier in the world—now addressing a market of well over 30 million front-drive vehicles built annually. In the early 1960s, it supplied fewer than 200,000 a year.

The other problem was the little tyres on the little wheels. The car used the Morris Minor's A-series engine and was ridiculously fast and quite capable of shredding drive-wheel tyres. They simply were not supposed to go round that fast. There were a number of so-called bubble cars on the roads of Europe, but these rarely exceeded 55 miles per hour, and Issigonis had specifically been told that the Newmarket must eclipse all such cars in speed. Interestingly, BMW was then a new company making the BMW Isetta bubble car.

The Isetta was introduced in 1955—just a year earlier than work started on the Mini at Longbridge. The Isetta's base price in Germany was the equivalent of £900 ($1,696.13 U.S.), and its 12-horsepower motor generated a ferocious 53 miles per hour. Dunlop was chosen to find the construction and compounds for tyres that would comfortably exceed 75 miles per hour, and it did, just in time. Within three years of the Mini's arrival, BMW halted Isetta production even though its popularity had generated 161,575 copies in seven years. It was to be the last time that BMW was

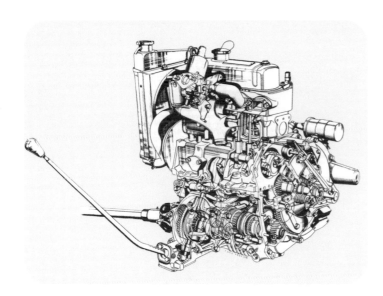

At the time, the Mini power unit was considered complex. This 1959 Theo Page drawing shows why. Today, nobody thinks twice about it.

subordinated by the British motor industry, a fact that was reiterated in 1993 the day that BMW took control of what was then the Rover Group.

Tom French was in charge of the programme for the Dunlop tyre company in Birmingham. He remembers how the wheel size was first established at a meeting with Issigonis

The BMW Isetta bubble car predated the original Mini but lasted only a fraction of the time.

For road trials, the prototype Mini was disguised with an Austin A40 front end.

and teams of engineers from both sides. Issigonis had been single-mindedly pressing the point that too much of a car's interior was lost to the intrusion of large wheel arches. For illustration, he had a pile of five full-sized tyres and wheels by his desk. Someone eventually asked him what size he thought he wanted, and Issigonis held his hands aloft and spread them until he was satisfied with the dimension he was demonstrating. There was silence in the room. Everyone was astonished. The size had still not been established in a way that could be recorded. Eventually, one of the Dunlop team walked over to Issigonis' desk and picked up a ruler, which he used to measure the gap between the client's outstretched hands: it was 10 inches.

The Golden Opportunity Squandered

In 1959, BMC was the fourth largest carmaker in the world and regarded as the largest producer of small cars. The goodwill (and the control) induced by the outcome of World War II meant that the company had a near-captive market in some areas of the world. All it had to do was to treat customers with respect, and the cash tills would never stop ringing. As things turned out, the Brits—like the Americans—preferred to adopt a contemptuous attitude to the export market for mass-produced cars and, over a matter of only three decades, allowed the underdogs from Germany and Japan to seize all the prizes.

By August 26, 1959, the date of the official unveiling of Mini, versions under the names of Morris Mini Minor and Austin Seven had been delivered to showrooms all over the world. Both names had resonance. The original Austin Seven was launched in 1922 and was a phenomenal success matched only by the Model T Ford. The Seven was also a foundation stone for the Japanese motor industry in that the patents to it were eventually sold to the Nissan Motor Corporation. The Morris branding was retained to emphasise that this car was a stable mate to the Morris Minor—then the most refined of the mass-market cars in the UK, a huge success, and held in great affection by its owners. A thriving professional restoration business exists to this day.

In inflation-accounted terms, the Mini Minor was to be sold more cheaply than the two-seater Morris, which had sold for £100 ($188.46 U.S.) in 1931. The base price had been fixed at £496 ($934.76 U.S.).

Ford was the big rival at that time and was selling the relatively antique Ford Popular for £419 ($789.64 U.S.). John Barber, a very experienced accountant at Ford who later took charge of BMC, admitted to being astonished on Mini launch day. He could not believe that this great little car, so crammed with innovation, would be priced so cheaply. Every daily paper that morning carried full-page BMC ads that flaunted just how much was new. The emphasis was on the front-wheel drive, the fully independent suspension, a top speed above 70 miles per hour, and a fuel consumption of 50 miles per gallon at 50 miles per hour. The fuel prices of the day allowed the calculation that the cost at that average speed was a penny a mile.

In the 1960s, the Mini men tried all sorts of ways to make the Mini bigger and worthy of a bigger price. This Clubman front was adopted; the tail end was not, thankfully.

Opposite Page: The 9X proposed Mini replacement got as far as becoming a runabout for Issigonis. It is photographed here in the great man's drive in Birmingham.

Designer Dick Burzi discusses the finer points of the proposal from Farina, the Italian styling house. This was code name 9X.

Left: XC for "experimental car." This was the rear of the Mini prototype running test car.

Everybody loved the Mini Stretch. It took Mini to the next size up and had elegance, but it was never made.

The ride was described as the silkiest possible; the cornering like that of a sports car. There was plenty to excite the enthusiast, but the emphasis was on how cheap the car was. And as things turned out, that was a huge mistake.

Issigonis was partly to blame; his early life as a political refugee supporting an elderly mother made his tastes and habits extremely frugal. While he was putting together his minimal car, he came to believe that he would be the friend of financially challenged, marginal motorists the world over. But he wasn't. The economy-minded motorist is averse to risk and doesn't want to be told how much innovation there is in a car. And salesmen don't like dealing with the impoverished, because the sale takes too long.

The middle class of the day should have been the target, and they would have paid up. After all, the newly launched Triumph Herald was selling for £796 ($1,500.13 U.S.) without offering any better legroom. (Mini legroom was identical to that of the average American car of the day.) The top speed, fuel economy, and acceleration of the Herald were all inferior. Only the Herald's legendary turning circle was a cut above; regardless, buyers spurned the Mini because it was too cheap. Sadly, the guiding principle of the car market in those days was that large and expensive were inseparable. Cheap and small were also words packaged together. Those who did buy Minis got sensational performance very inexpensively. Initial sales were worryingly slow.

Then to the rescue came the rich and fashionable. London, in those days, had no parking bays, and the man with the shortest car got the last parking space at the roadside. Such luminaries as the Beatles, Princess Margaret with Lord Snowdon, Peter Sellers and Mary Quant, Harry Secombe, and Graham Hill were seen around town in Minis, weaving in and out of the fast-moving traffic on Park Lane and diving into parking slots as short as 11 feet 6 inches at the pavement edge. The smoking front tyres, the bellow of the Peco exhaust, and the whine of the Mini gearbox in the sump combined to announce the arrival of the young, wise, wealthy, and adventurous.

Eighty lucky motoring journalists of the day got Minis on long loan. It wasn't simply a cynical attempt to generate an obligation; the benefit to BMC was that Minis turned up to every race and major event in the motoring calendar.

For a while, the Mini "hovered on the brink of failure," according to the wisdom of the day. There were too many faults: the clutch often failed, the early gearboxes had several flaws, and one of the metal plates in the subframe had been designed to weld the wrong way round, which caused a serious problem that took a while to emerge. Because Mini was launched at the height of summer, the severity of the water leak in the floor did not show up until the roads were awash with winter rains, and by then there were

20,000 cars on the roads of Europe. Before long, the cabin of a Mini was distinguished by the smell of rotting carpet. Competitors would advise customers also considering buying a Mini to ask for the free pair of BMC Wellington boots.

At Last There Was a Four-Seater Cheap Enough for Motorcyclists to Be Able to Come In From the Rain

After so poor a start, many cars would have sunk without a trace, but Mini was saved by its personality, if it can be reasonably argued that cars can possess such a quality. Because Mini was so round, cuddly, small, and vulnerable, owners—and especially female owners—developed a parent/child relationship with the car rather than the more common adult-to-adult relationship in which the car owner expected responsible and dependable behaviour. By the time Mini was in its 13th year of production, it had become the car of choice for women, and a Mini was as often as not the first new car for the female buyer. Half of all buyers that year were women.

For the girls, the attraction was as to a baby. The boys, on the other hand, wanted to alter this thing in their own image and thrash it to within an inch of its life. Many of them had come indoors from a motorcycle or motorcycle-and-sidecar combination, and they wanted to get as much fun as they had in the past. Just because a four-seater was at last affordable, it didn't mean it had to be dull.

The enfranchisement of this breed of young males had two instant effects. One was the near-total destruction of the British motorcycle industry, which rolled on its back and let the Japanese take the game to newly emerging motorcycle markets all over the world. The other was the creation from scratch of the motor accessory industry. Suddenly, all over Britain, there were corner-shop boutiques devoted to cosmetic personalisation and go-faster goodies.

And it was more than just a do-it-yourself craze. A highly professional mini-industry grew up around engineering and coachbuilding wizards, such as Daniel Richmond of Downton, Ralph Broad, Harold Radford, and, of course, the late, lamented John Cooper. The Hillman Imp and the Ford Anglia, which were also coming down the chute when Mini appeared, contributed to the DIY performance craze. But it was Mini that spawned it.

Opposite Page: This was a tricky photo shoot. *The Daily Express* newspaper wanted to celebrate the British Mini success. It took 804 Corgi model cars to plan the layout of the real thing.

Chapter 2
BL to BMW

By the 1960s, Austin and Morris were working together as BMC. In 1968, British Leyland (BL) was created by merging BMC with the Leyland truck company. This agglomeration was as fruitful as mating a steeplechaser with a dray horse. The once-proud but financially distressed Jaguar, Rover, and Triumph were all part of the shambling organisation. By 1975, it went bust and was nationalised. In 1979, Honda secured a 25 percent shareholding in BL, accompanied by technical collaboration on both cars and engines. The relationship with Honda was nurtured personally by British Prime Minister Margaret Thatcher, who came perilously close to letting the company go under.

The outright owner of Rover at the time of the BMW takeover in 1993 was British Aerospace, which had bought the stake owned by the British government, both to gain some asset backing for its own faltering business and to win political favours for the aerospace industry.

During the final days of the British Aerospace/Honda regime, the fate of Mini had been pondered long and hard. The car was by then down to production of 20,000

Above and Right: The first milestone came up after three years—December 12, 1962. The 500,000th new MINI took longer—August 2005.

a year, with nearly half of those being sold as antique curiosities in Japan.

There was no place for Mini within the collaborative venture with Honda, which had its own ideas as to what made a small car, and very good ideas they were, too. The Rover business wanted the space at Longbridge to manufacture six-cylinder versions of the faithful K-series engine.

500·000th
MINI

Researchers looked at the idea of selling the tooling to a third party and buying back cars. They wondered whether to license manufacture to a small-scale assembler. In their most delirious moments, they wondered if they could license a new business with the Mini name and encourage it to make all sorts of consumer goods with royalties flowing back to the distressed parent at Longbridge.

Mini Becomes Part of BMW

In 1994, BMW assumed control of the factory in Oxford that had turned out cars for Austin, Morris, AustinMorris, BMC, British Leyland, Leyland Cars, BL Cars, Austin Rover, and MG Rover. The various reincarnations marked the difficult journey of the British motor industry, which suffered from government intervention, substandard management, and rampant union power. By contrast, the German industry, which was restructured and revived after World War II by a British task force, powered out of poverty in an unswerving stream of performance.

Partly because of the history of rivalry and hostility between the two countries, BMW was tentative about its

Water testing became an unpleasant essential in the first few months of production.

Right: The BL Mini production was quite scattered. In Italy, not only was there production of the Cooper (left line) but also a fresh body style called the Innocenti.

Apparently, all this luggage will go inside, but probably not on the first try. Yet another promotion for the Mini.

Opposite Page: Ten years on, in 1969, Marketing Manager Tony Ham and his miniskirted friends launch the Clubman range at Longbridge. The doors were mounted on special lift-off hinges to show off the wind-up windows and new trim.

ownership of MG Rover. By 2000, BMW had had enough of financial losses and announced it was pulling out of Rover.

At that time, the Cowley plant (now retained by BMW for MINI and known as BMW Plant Oxford) was making the Rover 75 executive saloon, a very good car that handled brilliantly and was regarded as a successful car. But it was not a commercial success; the Rover brand was dying

despite very considerable investment from BMW. Those who worked at Cowley feared that the company would shut down for good when BMW left.

But there was another surprise to come. The remnants of the Rover group were to be bought by Phoenix, a private company that outmaneuvered Alchemy and which was to centre all its operations at Longbridge in Birmingham. Land Rover was being sold to Ford. Cowley was to build the new MINI. BMW therefore would hang on to that part of the British operation, and only that part.

As BMW was going through its final due diligence in Munich and deciding exactly how much it would pay, only one thing was certain about the Mini brand: at the age of 34, it was like a Premiership footballer. One more injury, and its playing days were over.

The barrel Mini design study aimed to replace the elbow room that was lost when the windows changed to wind-up from laterally sliding. The rear quarter was de-seamed.

Opposite Page: The greatest amount of thought to augment or replace Mini with something evolutionary was expended in the late 1980s. This is the four-door experiment.

No one could have guessed at the affection for the Mini that lurked within the beating heart of Bernd Pischetsrieder. He was the man running BMW at the time and championed the flawed strategy of expansion by acquisition. It was uncanny—not only did he believe that the Mini brand had enormous unexploited potential, but he also had Sir Alec Issigonis as a family member. He knew the man throughout his childhood as Uncle Alec.

In the mid-1990s, while the new MINI was still nothing more than code name R59 (R for Rover, 59 for the year of its launch), the car was expected to resume its historic place at Longbridge, where it would succeed the whole range of small Rover cars. The plan was that it would sell throughout the world through both BMW and Rover dealers. It was envisaged quite clearly at that time that it could sell at the rate of 200,000 a year, and only Longbridge could accommodate that volume. Or so they thought.

Manufacture was *briefly* considered for Cowley, although Pischetsrieder didn't want a MINI factory at Oxford. Mini was actually built there at the start and branded as Morris Mini Minor. But Pischetsrieder was adamant that Longbridge—the home of Austin in Birmingham—had become Mini's spiritual home and that traditions were too important to be tinkered with. He was very conscious also that there were people in the plant who had spent their entire working lives lovingly teasing Minis out of tired tools.

Pischetsrieder, however, would not be the man to decide. Six years after BMW bought the right to run affairs at Rover, there was still no MINI and, more fatally for Pischetsrieder, no money coming out of Rover. BMW shareholders and the controlling Quandt family wanted blood. On February 5, 1999, Pischetsrieder had to offer his resignation to the board.

The board accepted but still needed to find a strategy to save BMW from mounting losses and worsening relationships with its so-called "English Patient". There was no guarantee of a new MINI even though three design teams had been involved in trying to determine a winning formula.

The new man in charge was Joachim Milberg, a former engineering professor at Munich University. The board meeting that appointed him also approved a new MINI for production at Longbridge. The final piece in the jigsaw puzzle took several months to fall into place. It was actually more of an avalanche than a fall and was precipitated—not for the first time for British Leyland and its successors—by the British government.

BMW had splashed £2.5 billion ($4.71 billion U.S.) over five years on Rover by 1999. For the year 1997—a period beset by a very high value for the British pound sterling, which hampered exports and encouraged imports—operating losses were £650 million ($1.2 billion U.S.). The Germans had been proposing to bite the bullet and invest a further £1.5 billion ($2.83 billion U.S.), but first Her Majesty's Government had to put up a token contribution. A sum of £200 million ($377 million U.S.) was proposed and tacitly agreed to, but come the day, the BMW board was left looking at the offer of an emaciated £118 million ($222 million U.S.) phased over five years.

The sum was subsequently increased, but not back to the level of £200 million ($377 million U.S.). Worse still, the Department of Trade and Industry could not even confirm

The Mini Metro, which was launched at the 1980 UK motor show, could have looked like this had BL chosen to take the evolutionary-from-Mini route. Instead, it was decided to keep the original classic Mini shape in production, drop all derivatives, and introduce Metro in its own image.

Right: The Metro final design as tested in consumer clinics.

Right: Power brokers: Gordon Brown (left), Britain's Chancellor of the Exchequer, was at the end of the assembly line when the second-generation MINI started to emerge. With him was Norbert Reithofer, the newly appointed chief executive of the BMW group, who was the production man on the board when the decision to revive the Mini brand was made.

that the grant would be approved—as was required—by the European Commission.

The double-dealing on the amount and the doubt on the approvals triggered a sudden change of mood at BMW. Instead of being committed, the corporation wavered. On the very first day that a tentative buyer for Rover knocked on the door of the BMW offices in Munich, it swung welcomingly open.

That first inquiry was from Alchemy, a venture capital company of some repute. But when the time arrived for them to actually buy Longbridge and take it away, they were rumbled by Her Majesty's Government, which once again constructed an obstacle. In the person of industry minister Stephen Byers, it objected to the plan for a huge reduction of car production at Longbridge. That was the essence of the Alchemy plan. The managers imagined that Rover could make money on a much-reduced range of sports cars and sporting saloons bearing the MG brand. The consequence would have been thousands of job losses.

That impasse provided an entrée for John Towers, the man who had been managing director of Rover when British Aerospace sold it to BMW. He pulled a few pals together in great haste and, under the name of Phoenix, made a cash offer comparable to the Alchemy proposal, but with two huge distinctions. One was that he would keep the Mini. The other was that he would keep running the business as a volume car company with minimal job losses at Longbridge. That was what the government wanted to hear.

The jobs promise won him the company—even though BMW snatched back Mini at the last minute. But the final deal was that Rover 75 would have to move to Longbridge to concentrate all the Phoenix businesses on one site. That meant Mini would have to move to the site vacated, which was Cowley, Plant Oxford. The last piece of the jigsaw puzzle was in place. This plan suited BMW quite well, because all the initial investment to support the launch of the Rover 75 had gone into Cowley. Longbridge had been neglected while the future of the Mini and the Rover 200/400 range was settled. Longbridge's modernisation would never be met by BMW and indeed was never successfully arranged by John Towers and Phoenix. Instead, the rump of the British-owned motor industry fell into receivership in 2005, and its stricken production plants were picked over by a part of the emergent Chinese auto industry, Nanjing Automotive.

The Factory Swap

The day that BMW announced that it was keeping Mini, the senior people attached to the Mini business did not know whether to laugh or cry. Admittedly, the John Towers purchase of Rover at Longbridge looked a shakily funded operation that probably would not go the distance. But on the other hand, BMW was a retreating force that might well retreat again if things did not go well for MINI from the off. And as an organisation, it had no recent experience of small cars, though strangely enough, BMW's origins after World War I were as a producer of the BMW Dixie, derived from the tiny Austin Seven.

Paul Chantry was the senior Brit at Cowley tasked with managing the manufacture of the Rover 75. BMW ran Oxford as a manufacturing plant that answered to the head of BMW group manufacturing in Munich. There was no engineering in the UK. UK marketing had a big operation co-located with BMW UK at Bracknell, also answering to Munich. Cowley therefore was an overseas satellite plant for a German company. There had been little cause for personnel to mix with colleagues from Longbridge, the other overseas BMW manufacturing plant.

Chantry got a sniff that something funny was going on only shortly before news of BMW's sale of Rover. "I had a role in the plant in charge of future planning, and I started getting unexplained visits from Munich from senior people [who were] asking questions [and] could not discuss what the answers were needed for. It was clear that they were studying a range of options, and one option was the manufacture of MINI at Cowley."

Given that nearly all the MINI production tools were already installed at Longbridge and preseries production had already started, the questions were pretty odd.

The mystery lasted for two months; then came the announcement that Rover was gone, Land Rover was out, and MINI was moving south.

"I got a phone call a week later asking me to get together with my old friends at Longbridge and work out how we were going to swap MINI and Rover 75 over without losing supply of either car."

At the time, it was to be the biggest logistical problem ever managed by the British motor industry and with hindsight, it went extremely well.

Chantry pulled together a small team and, over a hectic 48 hours, came up with a plan. Cowley decided to go on making Rover 75 saloons until July 2000 with the assembly line running on a single shift and making 200 cars a day while the body shop ran two shifts a day. Within a couple of months, they had generated 6,000 Rover 75 bodies, which were shipped up the motorway by truck and stored in every available nook and cranny of the Longbridge site.

In July 2000, BMW hired a company to strip the MINI production plant out of Longbridge, while Phoenix hired an equivalent specialist to strip the Rover gear out of Cowley. All day long, the huge pieces of equipment passed each other aboard groaning trucks on the M40.

By September, all the equipment was commissioned in Cowley, and by December 2000, the new company with the year-old equipment was producing new-generation MINIs. However, the paint plant at Cowley had been specified for an executive car that was never going to sell in huge volumes. So although the BMW had originally seen MINI as capable of selling 200,000 a year, new MINI management had to admit to the press that the paint plant bottleneck meant that they could never build more than 100,000 cars a year. That the number manufactured exceeded 200,000 in 2005 is a story of extraordinary ingenuity.

The Overlay of BMW Quality

Unexpectedly, there were engineering changes to make to the MINI. BMW's supervision of Rover had not always been rigid—in fact, postmortems seem to agree that they were not rigid enough. Also, the MINIs were to have been sold under the Rover banner. With Rover gone, there was no intermediary enabling BMW to keep its distance. Once the company realised that the MINI would be reviewed as a BMW, it had to maintain its reputation by building the car to the standards applied to others bearing the BMW badge.

For nearly six months, there was no production at Cowley, and there were hundreds of associates with no work to do. Many of them took rapid training and helped pull down obsolete buildings and put up pretty trees. Hundreds of others went to Regensburg—ultimately the producer of the BMW 1 Series. All BMW plants have a twin to turn to for help and advice. Regensburg was to be Cowley's "marriage partner" plant—a kind of twin-town system that allows exchange of ideas and technologies.

There were several innovative actions taken by the MINI startup team. The first was shift patterns that had a series of different shapes. "It is like a gearbox," Chantry explained. "We have six shift patterns that we can select from, which give us all sorts of flexibility, including working twenty-four, seven if we want to."

The second was that a portion of associates should be agency-employed, so that if demand fell, the plant would not have to make its own staff idle.

The third was that there would be an hours bank. Hours worked could be rewarded by time off or extra holidays if that was what the individual wanted. Otherwise there were anti-social shifts on weekends and at night that commanded substantial hourly rate pay premiums.

There was innovation on the way the plant was organised—a whole basket of things called the New Oxford Way that changed decades of urban English tradition into BMW discipline. Things such as group management enabled everyone to be part of a group in which the members would manage their own holiday rotations. And there was scrutiny of management competence, increased speed of problem resolution, clear targets for all with appropriate training, and reward management.

Because the management team for the MINI transfer had to be set up so fast, Chantry had to draw on available

The bird's-eye view of the former Morris Mini Minor plant at Cowley near Oxford, which is now the dedicated home of BMW MINI and the world's only MINI assembly site.

managers from the German group. About 50 percent of the skilled managers were from Germany. This development gave way to an equal flow of Cowley's top talent across to Regensburg for training and wider experience.

Very soon, the problem was not getting the plant up and running, it was keeping up with demand. The response to the MINI launch had been that enthusiastic.

Chapter 3

Making It

Inside the paint oven at Plant Oxford.

When BMW said that it could only churn out 100,000 cars a year, that was based on an 80-hour week for the paint plant. Paint plants are sensitive and need plenty of shutdown time for purging and cleaning. Ovens have to be allowed to cool for that to happen. But with practice, the plant manufacturers' recommended throughput maximum was stretched to 134 hours a week.

There is another complexity in the MINI paint line in that the car often comes in two colours. John Cooper can be blamed for the troublesome and expensive refinement. His single-seat Cooper racing cars in the 1950s and 1960s always had a white stripe the length of the nose. When he got involved in Mini Cooper racing and rallying, his team signature initially was a white roof.

The white roof has stuck as a distinguishing feature of MINI Cooper, and at one time, 70 percent of the cars handled by the roof paint line within the paint shop had a roof paint option.

Luckily for the paint shop manager, it peaked at that point because of the introduction of the convertible MINI with its fabric roof.

What happens is that the roof gets a faint coat of body colour (the guns switch paint flow down as they go over a roof designated as white), and then the car gets diverted down a second run to get its whitening.

By the end of 2005, the plant had built 200,119 in the year. The new maximum capacity has become 240,000 for 2007, now that £100 million ($188 million U.S.) has been spent on an expansion of the body shop.

The rest of the capacity improvement has been earned by minute scrutiny of what was happening deep within the systems and then making engineering improvements. A very simple example was the reprogramming of the welding robots so that their jaws open on their way to the target, rather than travelling shut and opening on arrival. It saves a nanosecond, but added up over the year and multiplied by the total number of welds on each car, the time saving is huge and permits manufacture of extra cars.

Echoes of the Past

New MINI was a hard car to build, and therefore expensive.

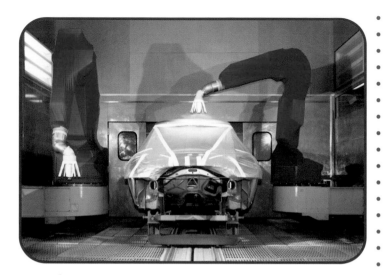

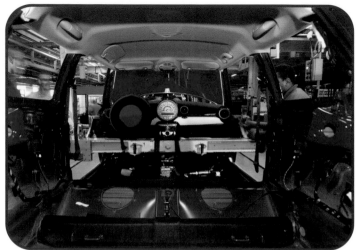

The roof painting needs its own sequence outside the main paint line.

It was clear that one of the pressures on designers was to keep the vital styling features that make MINI so reminiscent of Mini, to but engineer those features so that they could be manufactured more easily.

Did Plant Oxford ever have worries about building the car when it had so many elements that had never previously been encountered in an automated assembly hall?

"Plenty," remembers Chantry. Did he ever tell the Munich design team that the car could not be manufactured?

The near-naked shell of a second-generation MINI awaits its furniture.

Right: The complicated fitting of the convertible hood needs to happen offline at Plant Oxford.

"Product must take the lead. Manufacturing just has to find a solution."

The clamshell bonnet was a real manufacturing challenge because—regardless of the size of the vehicle—it is one of the largest that can be found anywhere in the world of car manufacturing. As the steel is pressed around the former, it is

Paul Chantry is the deputy director at Plant Oxford and the power behind the throne.

very difficult to ensure that the inner and outer dimensions of the steel remain equal. It needed endless trial and error to get it just right.

To get modern headlamps in the front without raising the bonnet height too much, the lamps had to be within the bonnet rather than the front panel of the car. That means that the clamshell lid becomes even heavier, requiring shock absorbers to prevent the bonnet from slamming down so hard that the lamps break.

With two struts at either corner, any slight difference in the resistance of one of them makes one corner of the bonnet panel flex. It was quite a challenge to ensure that the bonnet closed cleanly each time without breaking anything. "Twelve people spent six months getting that right," Chantry says.

The roof is a work of art. In the original Mini, the roof's gutter effect was actually a cheap external seam weld that was often a rust trap and a poor performer in aerodynamic tests. New MINI has a one-piece roof that mimics the original but sits like a lid over the body sides. To get it to sit right before welding, it has to be tapped in with hammers by an expert team. That costs.

Then there is the rear panel, which has taillamps set away from the boot opening—again an essential facsimile of the original Mini design cue. The small gap means a very difficult and expensive pressing for the rear panel.

Original Mini had a body stiffener behind the rear seat. MINI has nothing. The whole of the rear behind the front seats is open. The only upright between the front seat backs and the boot lid are the folding rear seat backs. But BMW insists on body stiffness to create the feel of a quality car and a quiet and controllable ride.

The appreciative German magazine, *Automobil Produktion,* said in 2001: "The torsional rigidity of the body shell is two or three times higher than competitors are able to offer. That means that under a torsional force of twenty-four thousand five hundred N-m, the body would twist only by one degree." In layman's English, that means that the body is so stiff it's quiet, because it is not prone to vibration; it is a safe passenger cell, and it has great directional stability when it is being steered hard into corners because it does not twist. Interestingly, MINI was one of the first cars to use a sophisticated computer simulation in development that meant that BMW did not have to twist and crush dozens of prototypes.

Lifting the Lid

A factory convertible came very late in the life of MINI, and BMW had not envisaged one at all. Classic Mini became converted late in life and had never been particularly convincing. But there was a group of keen young engineers in Munich, led by Siegfried Reichl and Josef Wuest, that was convinced that the ultra-stiff little car with its entirely open interior would make a great convertible car. Knowing that there was no official support for it, they just built one by scrabbling unused funds out of one research budget and another.

The convertible was eventually shipped across to Plant Oxford for the manufacturers to take a look at it. The presentation was done with some flourish, and the car was introduced as if at a motor show premier in the professionally lit presentation room within the administrative office block.

"They said what they had to say, and then waited," remembers Chantry. "We broke into spontaneous applause."

However, the convertible had additional manufacturing problems. The open deck area made it easy to stow everything away, but once the roof was removed, some of the torsional rigidity was lost. To regain it, the platform requires extra welds. In one area of the sill, there is 7 millimetres (0.039 inch) of welded material to compensate and achieve the correct rigidity. A huge amount of heat goes into that weld, which creates problems of its own.

There are some very complex lockdown mechanisms for the clever, automated hood. At the rear, the pram-hood-style lift and fold has to sit happily against the fold-down boot lid.

The Welcome Side to Manufacturing Complexity

Complexity at the MINI line side is the greatest organisational feat in the BMW Group. There are 3,400 parts to choose from, and they have to be delivered to the right point on the assembly line in synchrony with the car specified to take them. The MINI customer is positively encouraged to specify his own car, and so great now are the choices, that it is statistically unlikely that out of the 200,000 built in a year any two will be the same. Add the MINI line's run rate that is so far beyond design capacity, and the scale of the logistics achievement begins to become clear.

Plant Oxford was just beginning to think that there was no further scope for added complexity, when along came the John Cooper Works (JCW) derivative with requirements for Bluetooth, armrests, and many other details.

BMW is differentiating itself from other car builders with its can-do attitude. It likes to take an order from a customer well in advance of the required delivery date and then respond to calls for changes and additions right up to the week before the car is built. Experience shows that having dealt with the pain inflicted by the cost of the original order, customers can subsequently summon up the courage for a higher spec. The desire for air conditioning might be triggered by a hot day; the last-minute request for alloy wheels might be triggered by seeing a beautiful car in the street. That profitable upspeccing can go on throughout the waiting period and for as long as the ordering system can handle it.

Imagine the problem when Chantry's team has to decide on a Monday morning the order in which they will build the cars required that week. One way or another they are going to have to build over 600 cars a day, and there cannot be a stream of Cooper S versions, because the line speed would be too fast to handle the number of parts in each. And they can't be all colours of the rainbow, because the paint plant wouldn't have time to purge the paint guns often enough between cars. It's a great challenge, and the Plant Oxford boys have developed substantial admiration in other parts of the BMW Group.

There is an interesting cultural mix at Oxford, where, for a decade and a half prior to the arrival of BMW in 1994, Honda engineers were mixing freely with their joint-venture BL partners. MINI staff concedes that they learned a lot from the work practices of Japan but that BMW standards are far higher.

"We are proud of who we are," Chantry says. "We are MINI. We do things differently than BMW, and we do some things better. We like to say that we are a mix of English and German culturally. We are very good in a crisis. The German side is scrupulous in detailed planning and interpretation. We have a group of people who can take a risk on a measured basis. We will reuse facilities, and we will integrate new things.

"Our colleagues will ask guardedly: 'Are you sure you want to do that?' But if we had not taken those challenges, we would not have been able to grow as we have financially. Every year, we are tasked with significant cost savings; every year, we need continuous improvement; every year, we find some way to deliver."

Such is the fate of MINI men, and it was ever thus. Small cars take as many hours to build as big ones and are a hard row to hoe if the task is to spin a profit.

The first change of body shape for MINI—the remarkably successful electric-roofed convertible.

Chapter 4

Cooper's the Name. Speed Is the Game.

Opposite Page: The Spiritual was the car that the Rover engineers wanted to build. It was the BMW team that wanted to stay with the familiar Mini shape.

John Cooper, world champion race car constructor, died just before Christmas 2000. He'd seen the new car bearing his name. He'd reviewed the applause that had greeted its press showing in London and the public debut at the Paris Motor Show. He had driven a prototype MINI Cooper on the so-familiar drivers' roads around his south coast home near Worthing, UK. But he passed away before he could have any idea of the public demand for the second coming of Cooper.

Had anybody told him that MINI would become Britain's third-largest carmaker behind Nissan and Toyota, and ahead of Ford, Vauxhall, and Rover, he would have told them in no uncertain terms to lie down and take a rest.

But that was what happened. Within five years of going on sale, MINI was romping out of the Oxford plant at the rate of 200,000 a year, and the majority of the orders were for Cooper or Cooper S.

John Cooper had known about the BMW project to revive the small car for a very long time, as the German design team was punctilious about keeping him on side. There were concerns—big ones. Would the public accept a mixed-race MINI? Would Cooper want his name on it? Would BMW want Cooper to revive the relationship rather than go with M-power or Alpina?

The day it all came together, according to John's son Mike, was the day that he and his father went up to Gaydon, the secret Rover test track in the Midlands. The invitation was to look at a mockup of the car that had been selected to go forward to production in 1999. The Cooper men were not too excited on the journey up from the south coast. The previous attempts to recreate MINI had focused on packaging rather than performance.

They were thinking back to Spiritual and Spiritual 2, which had the engine under the floor and resembled a Mercedes A Class. There was also the ACV30, a Mini-ish roadster based on the MGF that made a brief appearance at a Monte Carlo Rally. It was quite a nice car, but it gave no clue as to what BMW might do with the base MINI.

They arrived at Gaydon and were shown to the presentation centre where many aspiring designers have nervously displayed their efforts over the years. Mike walked his

father into the room, and there in the far corner was a small vehicle. Surrounding it were the senior people from BMW development. There was a pause. John Cooper looked at the styling buck.

"It's a Mini," he said.

"All the people there were overjoyed," Mike remembers. "There was a tangible sense that the tension had been broken. My father was genuinely taken by the design."

It would be almost four years before the car would take to the streets in the hands of its proud new owners, and during that time Mike would be back to Gaydon to give advice on the behaviour of the performance MINI Cooper, launched simultaneously with the base car, MINI One.

"I wasn't sure about the steering at first. And it had no throttle response and no turn-in. I told them that it should have much more of the feel of a go kart." This was part of the consultancy programme that ensured that the MINI was the car that everybody wanted.

The Formula One Champ Adopts Mini

BMW was wise to keep the Cooper family close. In a strict commercial sense, there was no need to because, by a circuitous route, BMW had come to own the Mini Cooper name and could use it as they wished.

Charles Cooper, Mike's grandfather, founded the Cooper Car Company in Surbiton, a suburb of South West London, right after World War II ended in 1946. He lived to see the introduction of the original Mini derivative that bore his name in 1961, but died in 1964 as the Cooper S was being introduced. It was strange that son John should also die, at the age of 77, with the full knowledge that a BMW MINI Cooper was to be launched but without ever enjoying the fully developed S.

Charles Cooper was into motor racing, and John was in homemade karts powered by lawnmower engines before he was nine, and lapping Brooklands in things only slightly more advanced and entirely illegal by the time he was 14. The *Number One Cooper Special*, which was also built for John in 1935, used a highly tuned Austin Seven engine. By the age of 22, John was racing a prototype *Cooper 500* at the famous Prescott Hillclimb.

The GP is a strict two-seater with a stiffener across the rear.

Opposite Page: The whole name is Mini Cooper S John Cooper Works GP. The rear badging places "MINI" in the middle, "Cooper S" to the right, and just "Works GP" to the left.

Improvisation, experimentation, and ambition all became part of John's mindset. By the time he was 36, he was a Formula One champion car constructor, transported to the podium by Jack Brabham, who won the driver's title that year in a Cooper. Stirling Moss and Bruce McLaren were also in his cars that year. Between them, they crushed Porsche, BRM, Ferrari, Maserati, Aston Martin, and Lotus. And they did it again the following season. Not bad for a Surbiton garage man.

In John Bentley's book, *The Grand Prix Carpetbaggers: The Autobiography of John Cooper*, the great Ken Tyrrell described John Cooper as taking charge of the team that "did to Grand Prix Racing in 1959 and 1960 what Ferrari does today." Although that sentence about Ferrari omnipotence was written in 1977, it could equally have been written 25 years later.

Bentley also wrote of Cooper's dedication to the Mini and the extent to which his "unflagging enthusiasm and vision turned this little wonder car into a world bestseller."

John Cooper was no hero to Lord Stokes. The truck man, who took control of Rover and Triumph while running Leyland Trucks, merged the enlarged enterprise in 1968 with BMC, which by then had bought Jaguar. Stokes thought he had plenty of brand names without Cooper. He could not get past the problem that when Mini was generating little or no profit, he was giving the Cooper family £2 ($3.77 U.S.) a car.

Mike Cooper recalls Stokes asking his father what he actually did. John Cooper said, "I win world championships and go up to Longbridge once a week to wind up Issigonis."

Cooper and Issigonis both had an interest in motor racing, and the *Cooper 500* and the *Issigonis Lightweight Special* would be pitted against each other. But the two men talked often about engine development and suspension and handling innovation.

Cooper's rough handling of Stokes cut no ice in the business sense. When the prevailing five-year agreement with Cooper concluded in 1971, Stokes would not renew it. "Maybe it's because we did not go to the same school," John Cooper said laconically at the time. The official line that Stokes gave was that the Cooper name on the Mini badge depressed sales of the car because it generated inflated insurance premiums. In fact, the successor car—the Mini 1275GT—had a higher insurance group despite inferior performance. It was just another poor judgment by the BL board, which by then was but four years from achieving insolvency for the company.

Mike Cooper was born in 1954 and remembers a house full of parties and a garage full of Minis. Twelve was the record. "I really enjoyed my teenage years. I had a father who was a world champion and Steve McQueen staying over in my bedroom. Eric Clapton went to school three doors up from the garage, which was always full of rock stars."

The big change in life came in 1962, after John had a massive accident in the experimental twin-engined Twini Mini at 100 miles per hour on the Kingston bypass.

The rear tie rod broke, and the car went end over end, throwing John Cooper clear on its final somersault. He nearly died. Charles Cooper was certain that he was going to. John needed nursing and received it out of London on the south coast, near Worthing. He was fully repaired physically, but spent the rest of his life with angry headaches.

The red-bodied mirrors and GP graffiti up the nostril are the frontal clues.

Opposite Page: (Main) GP has a very distinctive side profile, with a modest spoiler perched on the back of the head.

(Inset) A close-up of the spoiler.

It was two years later that Charles, his father, died, and a still slightly infirm John Cooper began to get that end-of-an-era feel. At the same time, he was introduced to Jonathan Sieff, heir to the Marks & Spencer fortune, who had begun collecting car companies and garages. Cooper had an opportunity to sell his race car company for £250,000 ($471,148

The fastest yet—the John Cooper Works GP kit can be built on the assembly line or retrofitted by a dealer.

Left: Mike Cooper and Dr. Anton Heiss (foreground), head of the Oxford MINI plant, check out the installation of the first John Cooper Works tuning kits on the assembly line.

U.S.) but retain a job with the St. Michael Formula One team as technical director. The deal was done. John invested the money wisely in property, buying a garage at Ferring, near Worthing. The race game continued.

After four years, M&S had burned enough shareholder money, and folded the business. John bowed out of Formula One and picked up again with Mini Cooper racing.

"Dad got bored after a few years, and I suggested that we run the Ferring garage ourselves," says Mike. By then, he was an apprentice mechanic at Gray & Rowsell, the Ford and Reliant dealer in nearby Arundel.

Father and son started up initially in 1971 as a stand-alone Mini dealer. By coincidence, it was the year that British Leyland ended the use of the Cooper name. Then John and Mike took on the franchise for all BL cars. When the Mini Metro was launched in 1980, the Cooper Garage decided that it might offer the unpromising little machine as a Metro Cooper. It was warmed over with twin carbs in partnership with Janspeed and made to look the part.

"BL took a look at it and said that they were not interested," says Mike. "The next thing that happened was that BL announced an MG Metro with an engine that had exactly the power rating of ours and our choice of alloy wheels."

The Cooper story looked like it might be grinding to a halt. Then, out of a clear blue sky, came an extraordinary opportunity. Down the road in Worthing was the UK head-quarters of Nissan, which hired a huge tonnage of ships every year to float its cars over to the UK from Japan. Octav Botnar, the principal of Nissan UK, did not like the waste of sending all those vessels back empty and, by degrees, started filling them up with anything that might turn a profit in the Orient.

On one occasion, Botnar's people bought John Cooper's personal Rolls-Royce Silver Shadow—a car that he loved and maintained in pristine condition. He was per-

Mike Cooper with his famous father, John. Within a couple of years of this picture, dad had him driving on circuits.

suaded to part with it by an exceptional offer. Some used Minis were also shipped out alongside it.

"One day, the clear blue sky yielded a phone call from the BL agent in Japan who said that he wanted us to Cooper a Mini," Mike Cooper recalls. "We took a one-litre Mini Mayfair and dropped in a 1275GT. We upgraded the brakes and wheels and asked Rover to ship it out for us with their cars. They refused. So we smuggled it in through friends at Jaguar.

Mike Cooper with a classic Cooper against the historic background of single-seater racing.

Right: The birthplace of JCW tuning kits.

"Rover Japan loved it, showed it, and ordered 1,000. But Rover HQ again said that they were not interested and stamped on the whole project."

The project was kept alive by the unlikely intervention of a magazine publisher who said that what was needed was a retrofit tuning kit that could be shipped out. He said that it should be in a nice wooden shipping box that the customer could use as a coffee table and amuse his friends. The box would also be needed to house the unauthorised parts once a year, when they were stripped out of the car before it was submitted for its annual roadworthiness certificate. Once done, the kit would be refitted.

The trade went stunningly well. Hundreds of young Japanese motorists happily sat drinking sake around an empty wooden crate stencilled with the John Cooper name.

Cooper Embraces Honda

In the UK, the Coopers were doing their best to sell BL cars through their Ferring dealership, but were increasingly becoming concerned about the deteriorating quality of the products. One BL model stood out from the rest, and that was the Triumph Acclaim—made under a joint venture arrangement with Honda.

That year, at the 1987 British Grand Prix, the Coopers met up with Nobuhiko Kawamoto, chief engineer of Honda, whom they knew well. He had bought a rear-engined Cooper racing car in 1961, which had persuaded Honda to race with a car similarly configured. Kawamoto introduced the pair to the head of Honda UK. They told their tale about the quality of BL.

"On Monday morning, when we opened up, there were three Honda men on our doorstep."

By Tuesday afternoon, they had signed up for a Honda dealership. By Tuesday night, they were in Japan on a dealer trip that just happened to have been arranged for that day months earlier.

Mike Cooper recalls, "The final straw for my Dad with BL was when this 19-year-old regional sales rep had come in and told Dad that if we wanted to be able to order some new model or other, we would have to take four Rover SD1Ss. He then told my father—the former world champion—you have until three o'clock this afternoon to make your mind up."

Three years after the Cooper tuning kits were first introduced to Japan in 1986, they were still going strong, and one day BL was back on the phone wondering whether there was scope for a Cooper tuning kit in the UK. They came up with three flamboyant body styles: the Mini Racing, Flame, and Checkmate, all with Cooper's performance tweaks.

Further discussion established that to meet future emissions regulations, BL would have to use the 1275GT engine for all versions of the Mini instead of the antiquated 1-litre. So late in 1990, BL produced a limited edition of 1,000 cars with John Cooper's signature on the bonnet—they sold out overnight.

At that time, Tozer, Kemsley & Millbourn (TKM), a British chain of car dealers, held all the auto retailing assets that had been collected by Marks & Spencer. The Cooper name was included among the assets, so a royalty fee of around £20 ($37.69 U.S.) a car went to TKM—subsequently bought by Inchcape plc, another UK-listed car retail group—rather than the Cooper family. TKM, and then Inchcape, used the Cooper name on some of its showrooms. Those garages were used to sell BMW cars. That is how BMW and Cooper names came to be linked, long before BMW bought BL or recreated the MINI Cooper.

The Downbeat Decade

Throughout the 1990s, there followed a succession of technology changes for Mini engines, as fuel management was chased through several stages of development required to meet emissions legislation. Cooper kept up with the factory changes with a succession of tuning kits that derived better performance from the single-point and multi-point fuel injection in both Cooper and Cooper S forms.

In the end, the final model years of classic Mini production, right up to the year 2000, were Mini Coopers. The Mini Mayfair—the name synonymous with the high-trim level—was dropped in favour of the performance name.

By chance, Mike discovered in 1999 that the Cooper Car Company name was no longer registered, and it is now back in family ownership—as is the roundel, the Cooper badge, which has been registered as a trademark of the Cooper Car Company.

Cooper's Honda business had also been growing. Fittingly—given their performance history—the Coopers decided that they could become a specialist with the Honda NSX sports supercar and turned themselves into the biggest NSX dealer in Europe by trading in used cars as well as new.

"But in the end," says Mike, "the dealership became just another volume-driven business. As soon as Honda built its factory in the UK, we were back under the cosh having to process a predetermined volume of cars."

The Ferring business was sold and the Honda franchise with it. In 2006, it changed hands again and became a Vauxhall dealer in the ownership of the Frosts group, which specializes in the Vauxhall marque in the locality.

Close formation from a matching pair of racers.

The Cooper business became centred on an out-of-the-way showroom and workshop site near Ferring at East Preston and at a warehouse on an industrial site a mile away, which handles retail orders for the Cooper parts and tuning kits worldwide.

East Preston was a smart, modern facility that had historic Cooper single-seaters nestled alongside personalised performance MINIs, and many showcases around the walls contain the trophies and memorabilia of the last 50 years. In the workshop, behind a glass partition, were classic Minis in varying stages of restoration, many of them cherished possessions of members of the Cooper family.

At the end of July 2006, the dealership closed when Mike decided to get out of retail to concentrate on tuning kits—now all available as a factory fit or retrofit by a MINI dealer.

Cooper Joins the BMW Family

When the Cooper relationship with BMW started to grow, it was a very welcome new business stream. Mike was asked to be an ambassador for the MINI brand and a consultant on the preparation and presentation of factory cars bearing his name. That was all in parallel with the role of building Cooper tuning kits for new and classic Minis.

Mike began publicly driving a new BMW MINI Cooper while about his normal business in Sussex as early as 1988. "I knew it was going to be well received; whenever I parked it, there would be 100 people round it when I came back."

The first kit from Cooper was an enhancement of the basic MINI Cooper car that boosted the brake horsepower from 105 to 130. But then when the factory Cooper S came out, the brake horsepower was taken all the way to 165. It went up again in 2003 to 170 horsepower. "When we looked at the opportunity to tune that one, I immediately wanted to head for two hundred bhp," Mike says.

"There was a good technical reason. The noise regulation makes a step change at that point and allows a two-hundred-bhp vehicle to make more noise than one that is below one hundred ninety bhp. We wanted a really good 'drive-by' noise from the Cooper S to give it a supercar sound. We decided to do two things: to spin up the supercharger and give it extra pressure, which meant fitting a smaller pulley wheel. We then ported the cylinder head for inlet and outlet valve improvements."

The technical adviser and designer for Cooper tuning kits was Mike Theaker—formerly with Aston Martin and Ricardo Company—whom Mike regards as one of the best power engineers in the world.

Cylinder heads were made by Swindon Race Engineers, and the exhausts for the kit were made by CLF Technology, which also supplies to Lotus and Aston Martin. There is no performance improvement gained from the choice of exhaust, just an improvement in the engine noise by tuning the way it sounds. There had to be a lot of testing of the kits at high and low temperatures and with all grades of fuel, including the lowest that it was possible to encounter.

Chapter 5

The Man Behind the Brand

Opposite Page: Vice president, brand management MINI is what it says. What it means is that Kay Segler is the boss of the worldwide operation.

Kay Segler (pronounce it Kie) leans forward and says, "Believe what I am telling you. MINI is a *very* masculine car."

It sounds a trivial point. But in branding terms, it isn't. Once a car develops a feminine cachet (as did the revival VW Beetle with the engine at the wrong end) the potential market is immediately down by half. The ladies are okay about buying a man's car. It doesn't work so well the other way around.

Segler is the man who runs MINI worldwide out of Munich and who launched the new MINI at the end of 2006. He has been vice president of MINI brand management for two years and hopes that he will be in charge of the car's development for many years to come.

He is one step below the BMW main board and answers to Dr. Michael Ganal, the group director of sales and marketing. MINI manufacturing at Plant Oxford reports to the main board through the group manufacturing director, Frank Peter Arndt. It used to be Norbert Reithofer in that position. He is now the newly appointed CEO of the BMW Group and therefore carries affection for the MINI

into the heart of power. Legally, MINI is only a virtual company. On paper, it has no independent existence. In reality, it has huge freedoms.

What Segler loves about the job is being in on the ground floor of a new brand. Of course it is new, and then it isn't. MINI has been around for six years. That's new compared with other automotive brands. But classic Mini was conceived when Issigonis first put pen to paper more than 50 years ago. For those who enjoy the tidiness of round numbers, the centenary of Issigonis' birth was November 18, 2006. He was 50 years old when he sketched the cherubic face of Mini.

Segler was talking about his plans the day before his own 51st birthday. He's a BMW careerist who has done corporate planning and overseas staffing. Prior to his placement at MINI, he ran BMW Asia from Singapore and spent five years on a variety of after-sales functions.

Segler likes to be confrontational, but his eyes are always smiling and there is always a crease playing around the corner of his mouth. He even has an argument for the

virtue of being argumentative: "Issigonis had the will to make the Mini happen. He insisted that his design was right, and he would not change it. You have to be courageous to get what you are sure is right. It is still true today."

BMW has had the sense to see that if MINI isn't different it will not be able to cast a long shadow. That is why so many of the MINI people strut about in BMW buildings muttering to themselves under their breath, "MINI is different. We do things differently." With no place to call home, no group headquarters, no corporate excess, and no flagpole, the MINI challenge is to stand apart and stay focused. Segler has Issigonis-like qualities and can provide the leadership that MINI needs to keep the show on the road.

So what sets MINI apart from the rest of BMW?

It starts in Munich. It's a no-ties dress code, of course. And the meeting room has stand-up desks to keep the meetings short. Another area has foam cushions to force people to sit in a different way and therefore think in a different way. In the UK, there is table-football to let people vent frustrations.

Once every year in the UK, there is a big strategy bash. The virtual company board consists of Segler, the head of engineering, the manufacturing chief, and the heads of sales in the big markets. Then there is the A-team that gets together every two or three months, including a conference call to those outside Munich. All operating decisions are taken at a heads-of-function meeting every couple of weeks.

Opposite Page: The spectacular paint jobs applied to MINI have been preserved in an exhibition at BMW headquarters in Munich.

The way in which headquarters interfaces with MINI dealers is an example of the way that the company thinks. Dealers are ranked by their success in selling additional features to customers. Rather than reporting back to dealers on where they are relative to the average, Segler gave them all a leader board to hang on the wall so that they could move themselves up and down the ladder with each new piece of information. It's more open, more competitive, more fun. And it helps sales.

You Only Get One Chance to Create a Harmonious Culture for a New Brand

Segler is very conscious that the BMW brand—strong though it is—is fragmented by the traditions that have grown up over the decades in the varying territories. And even though BMW itself remains a fabulous success story, the dealers do not share proportionately in that financial success.

"The dealer aspect is so often forgotten, yet every second day a dealer somewhere in the 70 MINI markets worldwide is making an investment of some sort in their facilities," Segler explains. "It has to be done right. We have to be involved. We have to help.

"One of the guiding principles of the company is that it will not launch derivatives selectively. Once a new car is available, it has to be available in all markets," Segler reckons. That means that there will always have to be sufficient volume to allow all of the 70 countries to get at least a handful of the newest cars.

"Dealers have a heart and a mind, and it is a hell of a job to help them get it right. It is as difficult as the problem of increasing assembly capacity." One of the great surprises is the international spread of demand. The United States and the UK head the list. Germany is third. Japan was always big for classic Mini—in the later years of Mini's life, Japan took more than half of the cars produced at Longbridge and cherished them as classic cars that just happened to be freshly minted.

But in Hong Kong, MINI is taking two percent of the market, which is extraordinary. And in Korea, where there is no Mini history whatsoever, the first allocation of 770 cars in 2005 sold out in nine months. The only connection for MINI in China was the Mr. Bean television series. But again, there is phenomenal interest.

In Brazil, where there is no import business yet, as is still the case with India, grey-market MINIs are changing hands at $50,000.

The average transaction price of a MINI worldwide is more than $20,000—50 percent more than the average for a Polo and often close to the price of a Golf, also a premium car in its sector but a whole size up.

The symbols of global success from Oxford to London, New York, and Sydney, Australia.

Some people in the organisation thought that if there was no MINI history in a market there would be no sales demand. They were very wrong.

The First Premium Car in the Small-Car Market

What does Segler see as unique about the product that he asks dealers to treat in such a special way?

"Go back twenty years. A premium car was always a large car. With all the gizmos that were needed inside, the big saloon was easier to build.

"The MINI is the first small car to say 'premium.' It is postmodern. Nobody understood that it could be achieved. Packaging is difficult, but we have achieved it. We have sold a lot.

"For me, the MINI is a kind of a muscle car. It has a lot of compressed energy. As a boy, you always wanted more power than you could control. The Cooper S has it. The Cooper S is very male, therefore, and at the heart of the brand. In concept, it has similarity to the Porsche: small, premium, too much power, sex appeal."

Product is the real substance of any business, and there has been more development of that substance within MINI than might be readily apparent. The job started with MINI One and MINI Cooper. Then came the Cooper S and the diesel using the Toyota Yaris engine. In 2005, the automatic Cooper S was introduced, mainly on the say-so of Asian and U.S. markets. The One and the Cooper had offered CVT from 2002. Then came the upgrade of the man-

ual box and the John Cooper Works (JCW).

At the Geneva Auto Salon in March 2006, MINI showed the John Cooper Works GP with a distinctive body kit, a brace bar in place of the rear seats, distinctive red door mirrors, and, of course, yet another increase in power output.

Most of the 2006 changes for the new MINI were driven by legislation. The company is very happy with the body shape and would not tamper with it if it didn't have to. Segler says that, from a market perspective, there is no need to change at all. Ask the owners what they think, and they say the car is still very fresh. Prospective owners never say that the car is dated. The discounts given on the car are still minimal. In Germany, discounts are actually reducing. Segler bought a MINI himself at the start of 2005.

"I will never sell that car. I think it will always be a classic fresh look."

But new pedestrian safety standards require tweaks to the front-end sheet metal that change the profile very slightly. The new engine sits slightly taller than the Tritec, and the latest pedestrian safety legislation means that the bonnet has to crush when struck by a pedestrian in an impact. therefore, there has to be a gap between engine and hood, which puts the MINI front a little higher again.

The 2006 change from the Tritec engine, built in Curitiba, Brazil, to the joint-venture unit design with PSA Peugeot Citroën has two aims: it has to be more cost effective, and it has to be more fuel efficient. BMW has a strate-

The new Cooper S turbo engine lurks below the higher bonnet line.

Opposite Page: The Porsche 911 of 40 years ago is a timeless shape that forms the coordinates of the 911 of today. It is the car that most influences BMW in its careful evolution of MINI. *Patrick Paternie*

gic advantage in including MINI it its group, as it contributes to reduction of corporate average fuel economy (CAFE) legislation. So while the bigger and heavier cars with bigger engines and greater performance at the top end may pull average fleet fuel economy down, MINI at the bottom pushes it back up.

So has the advertising programme for MINI been a big help; the endearing MINI adventure stuff that has famously been appearing in the UK?

"I *hate* the word advertising," Segler says. "It creates the sense that you are dressing something up. To me, MINI is its own advertising. Everything connected with the MINI should be integral. The buying of it, the living with it, and the communication about it must all be MINIed. There will be a verb of course. It will mean to do things the MINI way."

In the beginning, MINI had to piggyback on BMW dealerships to get started. But more and more often, the BMW logo endorsement is evaporating. The MINI shop in the Habitat store in Singapore has no logo. In the UK, more and more of the dealerships are solo.

"We are going to build a kind of a place where you can discover what MINI is," says Segler. "We would like to make it in the UK. Maybe Oxford."

"You mean a museum?"

"We are *not* building a museum." Segler looks fierce as he parries the words that cannot yet be part of the MINI culture. "It is history, but every day we are making our history. Each day we create more of the heritage." He smiles.

Chapter 6
The Man Behind the Style

Gert Hildebrand was a member of the Inzlingen wrestling club as a lad. He was also a stalwart of the village hammer-throwing club. He joined these groups because he was a sportsman and because Inzlingen is a tiny village in the southern tip of Germany close to the Swiss border. There were no sports facilities. His dad set up a sports club to do what could be done in the mountainous terrain. So Gert threw hammers and wrestled. Gert was throwing in the under 82-kilo class, and he was good. The village team became quite a success.

But Gert had a distraction. He had a teammate who travelled 150 kilometres from Bern, Switzerland, for every match. That guy was so cool. He had a white-roofed, light blue Riley Elf with all the chrome, tall radiator, the boot, and the fins. He would arrive in the village, open the boot lid, and there on a cushion was his hammer. So cool. To this day, Hildebrand wants a light blue Riley Elf with a white roof.

Hildebrand shared this illuminating elfin story at the 2006 Geneva Auto Salon. It demonstrates that Hildebrand is loyal to early enchantment and unafraid to admit it, despite the scorn routinely poured on the Riley corruption of the original Mini shape. That little detail of the hammer on the cushion is a true designer's observation. One can imagine a range of accessory cushions for the upcoming MINI Traveller (or whatever it will be called) in a range sized precisely for Labradors, hammers, or quail's eggs.

As he walked past MINI Concept Geneva—the third-showing-but-renamed concept car—Hildebrand was forever checking out the focus of the curiosities of the surrounding throng. Hildebrand is not likely to miss a trend in public taste or an unspoken desire from among the target audience of prospective MINI owners.

Without stretching the analogies further than they are prepared to go, Hildebrand's early-life experiences tell that, from childhood, he has been prepared to make the most of the facilities available. Though it has been a huge sales success, MINI is not a money fountain, point one. UK production costs and capped sticker-price potential for a small car make the economics tight. The issue of space in

A version of the car that set Gert Hildebrand's mind in motion. And it's for sale.

a small car becomes harder to deal with as the options list expands, point two.

Wrestling his way through those difficulties has become a daily event for Hildebrand. Building show cars which have huge research value, and serve as good PR tricks and brand advertisement—takes a great deal of time. As head of design, Hildebrand has a team of 32 designers but admits that they had sleepless nights and long weekends at the office to get the car ready for the Geneva show, alongside the daily grind of readying R55 and R56.

Hildebrand has been around a bit, but reckons that he has one of the best jobs in the industry. Five-and-a-bit million people worldwide bought a new classic Mini in the 40 years it was on sale. That's not a bad band of loyalists with

whom to develop what is effectively a new brand. "Mini was always connected to a positive image," he says.

Hildebrand is 52 now and has left his mark on a range of classic designs. Golf 3 was his watershed design, and he was the father of the new face of Seat. Audi 3 was also subjected to his influence. He was taken on by BMW in 2001, when he was invited to head a new design centre in Munich and tasked with designing the first MINI model change after the successful return of MINI in 2000. He gained a lot of his insight and knowledge from studying at the British Royal College of Art in London. Later in 2001, the MINI design team, initially located within the BMW Design Centre, moved to its new premises at Hufelandstrasse, around the corner from BMW's FIZ building, to get as much brand separation as possible and because the FIZ was overcrowded.

Partners in Design

Hildebrand worked briefly with Frank Stephenson, the man who is widely credited with settling the original design of the MINI and, interestingly, was born three months after the classic Mini first went on sale.

Because of his slight American accent, Stephenson is often described as American-born. In fact, he went to the United States to study at Pasadena's Art Center School of

Hildebrand at the Geneva Motor Show, showing the roof wheelmount of the Traveller concept car

Design. Stephenson was born in Casablanca. His father was a Norwegian, expatriate Boeing employee, his mother a Spaniard. Until he was seven, Stephenson spoke only French and Arabic. At 11, he recalls "freezing" when he saw a Ferrari Dino 246 driving down one of Casablanca's narrow, dusty streets. Like Hildebrand, he had been bitten by the bug that would shape his future career choices. He left MINI to go to Ferrari and the Fiat Group in 2002.

"After the success of MINI, the phone was ringing off the hook," Stephenson recalls. "One of the calls was from the 'godfathers' in Italy, with the offer I couldn't refuse."

Stephenson will be doing at Fiat what he did at MINI in part. Fiat used to be Europe's biggest provider of small cars, but the game has long gone to the Asian imports and other European makers. He has to reverse that loss and will to "play off the brand's historic treasures." The big news from Fiat is the return of the iconic 500.

"When I came in, the concept car was already there, so the project has really been about how we can make the 500 more desirable than the MINI," says Stephenson. "The MINI has set the bar upon which all the rest can be judged. It's the pinnacle of trendy cult cars.

"If you want to do something here, you have to pull customers away from [MINI]. Perhaps its greatest weakness is the price. This is where Fiat can succeed.

"The MINI was not a retro car. The new MINI was an evolution. I sketched out what it would look like in 1969 if they'd redone it, and then 1979 and up to 1999."

Stephenson applauds the performance of his former colleague Chris Bangle in having the courage to set BMW off in an innovative but highly controversial design direction, and he firmly believes that Europe holds the cards on car design: "American and Japanese products are not emotionally charged!"

Stephenson is a firm believer in personalization and predicts that the brand that offers customers the chance to

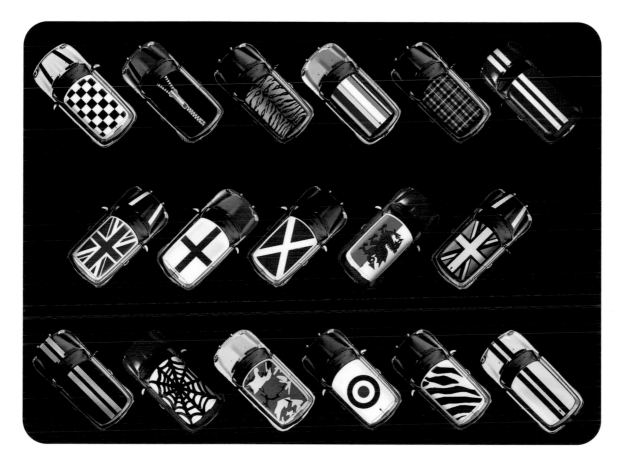

MINI is famous for
its topping style.

Gert Hildebrand with the MINI schematic.

Marc Girard at the big sketch board with Hildebrand to discuss cockpit options.

select unique colours, wheels, and interiors will reap the whirlwind. One of the innovations in the next MINI that he is pleased with is the ambience control: "You can make the people of Abu Dhabi feel cooler by offering a bluish tinge to the interior lighting. In Finland, when it is 30 below, you might want a warm red haze."

People buy the exterior appearance of a car but live with the interior: "If the interior does not convince, people will get rid of the car." Having adopted Stephenson's initial concept of new MINI, it is a fair bet that the company he has left behind will have embraced the concept of lively and innovative interiors.

Hildebrand acknowledges the role of his predecessor: "Stephenson did the key MINI sketch and then transferred his ideas to the final product."

Hildebrand likes to shatter the German reputation for modest skills in the management of humour. He jokes that the MINI job is ideal. "The old Mini lasted 40 years without change, so there is really little for me to do."

In truth, there is a great deal to do just keeping the little car in line with changing safety legislation, keeping the design fresh, and exploring the variety of potential derivatives. The thinking is clearly in the same channel as the thinking on other iconic cars, in particular the Porsche, Golf, and BMW 3 Series.

MINI was a no-brainer for BMW when, in 1993, it examined the portfolio of cars available to it for development in the Rover portfolio that it had acquired. It took seven years to get around to it because the English Patient needed so much lifesaving treatment in the medium- and large-car classes. The premium class was growing very fast worldwide in that period and so was small-car demand. It made sense to apply the BMW mastership of premium products to the small-car world.

"The car industry around the world is in deep trouble," Hildebrand says. "With every business success, product comes first. It is a really refreshing change for me to work with a brand that is so nice.

"The first success comes from good design. And the first design was a good one. It had form and proportion. Proportion is important and so is mimic and gesture—the way that a car 'mimics' human proportion and gesture, the way that it behaves in a manner that has recognizably human behavior. When the viewer looks at a car, he sees cues that have human equivalents. MINI is a child, but it has wide shoulders and wide stance with all four wheels at the corners of the car as a BMW has. This gives it the appearance of moving forward. Cars with a long front overhang look

Young interior designer Bruno Amatino gets his say.

static. The wide stance appeals to men's instinctive preference for a broad-shouldered demeanor. But it also has curves, which men like.

"It has coziness," says Hildebrand. "You want to hug it. It's like a teddy bear."

Women, meanwhile, are drawn to the car's cheerful front end and puppyish good looks, which make them want to nurture and mother MINI. It is appealing rather than intimidating, despite the overt overtones of speed and performance.

This is what Amatino and Hildebrand were looking at.

Dash designs are planned out full-scale.

"We must fight all the time to preserve the advantages we have won. Our design DNA must be un-copyable. If anyone else does the big bonnet with the lamps the way they are, that will be a copy," Hildebrand says. "We are the number one premium producer in the small-car business, and we must stay in front. That is the commitment for all the designers in the team.

"Issigonis did it alone. Today, if you have good people, thirty is enough. My role is to manage the team in a way that we can play that game and get the best results."

Hildebrand rules very little out when he contemplates the work ahead and the number of derivatives that might join the range. "The Moke was very good. Whenever I went on holiday to Greece, I would get one."

The Marcos sports car version of the classic Mini (developed by a company independent of BL) was also very good. The convertible has already been done. The Traveller lent itself to the first set of design concepts because it presented the option to increase available space, which is always tight in the base car.

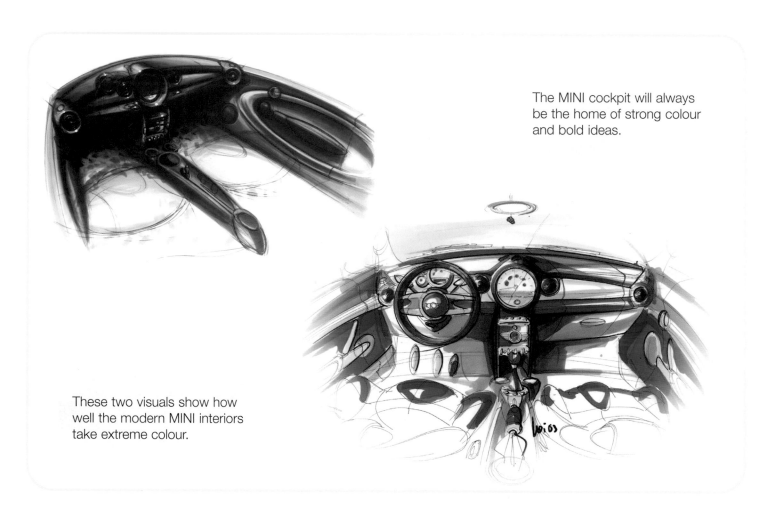

The MINI cockpit will always be the home of strong colour and bold ideas.

These two visuals show how well the modern MINI interiors take extreme colour.

The bonnet scoop on second-generation MINI Cooper S looked good in the drawings and stayed the distance, even though it was subsequently blanked off and has no function.

The single tailpipe marks this as a very late visual for the Cooper.

Suspension arrangements for MINI 2007.

"It is important to understand the thinking of Issigonis," Hildebrand says. "Today, we live in a world of luxury. In his time, there was hardship. He lost his father when he was very young. He lost his homeland and his childhood. He had to live with very little and learn to value minimalism. His achievement was that he was single-minded about producing a minimal car and refused to compromise. I admire people who stick with their ideas and with their goals to the end of their lives. He was stubborn. And I am stubborn."

New 1,600cc engine for 2007 MINI.

Opposite Page: The Tokyo Traveller has a tasty display of tea bags and spoons.

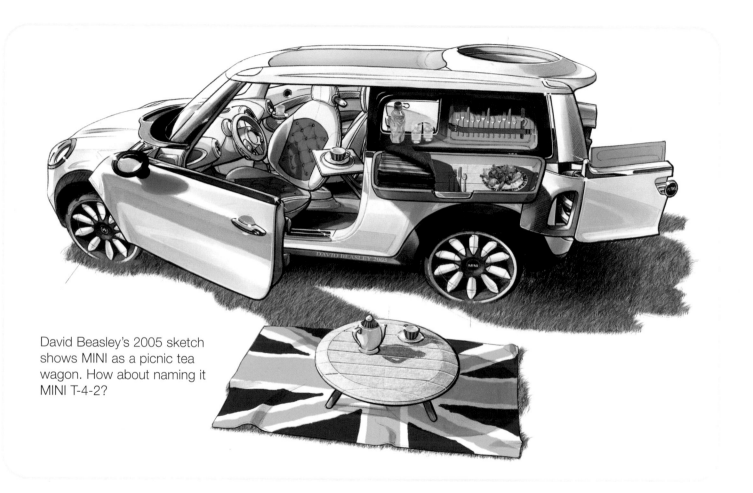

David Beasley's 2005 sketch shows MINI as a picnic tea wagon. How about naming it MINI T-4-2?

Above: The first, and comparatively plain, Traveller concept shown at Frankfurt in September 2005 has a pleasingly symmetrical rear with double doors.

Top Right: Front end of Frankfurt Traveller.

Bottom Right: The Ferrari racers and the model Fiat 500 buck on the desktop tell the story that Stephenson has moved on from MINI to Italy.

Chapter 7
Hello Again, Sir. Now What?

Opposite: Hams Hall is the newest of the three UK MINI production sites and has the best attempt at landscaping.

MINI has found the richest profit margin. It's the change-your-mind-at-the-last-minute layer of the profit structure. So determined is the German company to exploit the natural human tendency to vacillate, that it is moving factories around to accommodate last-minute consumer whims.

One example: BMW and PSA have embraced one another and a jointly designed 1.4- to 2.0-litre petrol engine. The machined components, such as the crankshafts, will be made near Lille, France. But while PSA will also assemble its versions on site in France, BMW is moving all its bits to Hams Hall near Birmingham in the UK, unpacking and assembling in its own engine factory. The new 1,600cc unit produces 20 percent better fuel economy with no loss in power outputs in its three stages of tune and has a slight torque improvement. BMW will not use the unit in its German cars. It will always be a MINI exclusive.

The Tritec engine was a joint venture with Chrysler, which was subsequently subsumed within Daimler Benz to create DaimlerChrysler. BMW always says that it does not have a problem dealing with its rival in Stuttgart, but BMW's actions in the past eloquently say otherwise. So it is no doubt with some relief to corporate anxiety that MINI is now in bed with those nice people in France.

The move of engine final assembly to the UK Midlands means that MINI becomes self-contained in the UK, with pressings from Swindon and assembly at Oxford all within 90 minutes of each other. MINI had the option of having its engines assembled at the same place that PSA does—Francaise de Mecanique in Douvrin, near Lille, France—but it prefers the UK. It makes better business sense to ship completed engines rather than engine parts, but BMW is now looking at the broader commercial benefits of manufacturing flexibility. The trip from Lille to the MINI assembly plant near Oxford is the best part of a day on a good day, worse if the roads are choked or the sea stormy. From Hams Hall, it's 90 minutes.

It may not seem to be much of a difference. But the man who makes engines for the MINI has been told by BMW that MINI customers can change on Tuesday the engine of the car that is being built for him the following Monday.

That's seven days. Not eight days, or even seven-and-a-half days, but seven. And the 90-minute journey that it takes for the engine to reach the assembly line therefore becomes a maximum.

Harald Krüger, managing director of Hams Hall, says that there is no doubt that the UK has a role in engine manufacture. Basic labour rates are not the highest in Europe, labour flexibility and labour skills are the best in the BMW group, and quality levels compare favourably with those achieved at the other BMW engine operations in Munich (Germany) and Steyr (Austria). Reliability and flexibility easily offset the 20 percent labour cost saving that might exist for BMW in Eastern Europe, and the proximity to the MINI assembly line means that customer preference for late changes of engine specification can easily be accommodated. That is a big competitive advantage.

It's the same with every component and in every BMW manufacturing plant worldwide—or will be. BMW is sufficiently well advanced with all this to have identified the last-minute spec change as a proposition of considerable commercial advantage. The pain of parting with money for a car softens while the excitement of waiting for it grows. And it is during that period that the buyer is susceptible to upgrading the wheels, fitting satellite navigation, going for the handling kit, etc. Had the handling kit been specified at the start, its cost would have been part of the initial price haggle. But when you ask for it to be fitted to a car being delivered next week and find that it can be made to happen, all the price resistance is knocked out of you and replaced by an overwhelming sense of gratitude.

It's not just factories that have to move to accommodate the seven-day lead time. Dealers have to be retrained to move to "certainly, Sir" from "you gotta be joking," and the IT network that reschedules a diesel instead of petrol engine to Monday's car number 1234/wow-uk has to be seamless and flawless.

The End of the Brazilian Connection

Hams Hall was set up in January 2001 and makes over 180,000 four-cylinder petrol engines a year and supplies them for BMW 1 Series and 3 Series, the Z4, and the X3. It exports to Regensburg, Munich, and Leipzig in Germany, to Graz in Austria, to its U.S. plant in Spartanburg, and to Rosslyn in South Africa. Design capacity of the plant is 400,000, so taking in the MINI petrol engine from Brazil will fill it. You can tell the MINI engines from the others as you look at the robots carrying them around the assembly hall because a transverse engine requires different pickup points.

By the end of 2003, the assembly hall hit all its profit and productivity targets, and by 2005, it had the highest quality in the BMW group.

One of the great positives for Harald Krüger, who runs Hams Hall, is the flexibility of the labour. He can run the plant from 30 hours to 142 hours each week without penalty from downtime or overtime payments. The staff members fix their own working hours to match the order process. And

Harald Krüger, the man in charge of making MINI engines at Hams Hall in Birmingham, England.

the staff members are multi-skilled so that they can shuttle from machining to assembly and back again to suit demand.

Krüger is very polite about the Tritec engine. The cost/performance ratio is very good, and the engine is considered unburstable by the racing fraternity, which has many war stories about unknowingly running without oil or water for long periods of time. But the Tritec was designed in 1997 and would not have met some imminent legislation details.

Hams Hall makes up the UK production triangle: Hams Hall to Swindon for body panels to Plant Oxford for assem-

It's another promotional MINI adventure.

Top right: The meeting of a cockpit and body.

Lower right: MINI swings in a cradle to ease underbody work.

bly. BMW is very happy about the concentration at last of all three factories. It creates for MINI and BMW, they say, a chance to prove that the UK is a world-class car manufacturing country.

Above: Parading through the paint plant.

Top right: Pop art from the bake oven.

Lower right: Some bits have to be reached by hand.

The marriage—body connects with soul.

Chapter 8
Mini and the Coachbuilding Tradition

Opposite: Every young man's dream in the 1960s was a Radford interior.

Marc Eden could not have been luckier. He was alone in the world headquarters of Radford one day when the e-mail came through. There on the screen was a man offering him one of the finest Radford Minis ever built.

Eden had tried his best to get away from Minis and from the coachbuilding business. He had even tried burying himself in the family business of retirement homes. But it was not going to happen. The lure of the fine motor carriage was too strong.

Eden's experience in coachbuilding goes back to Wood and Picket and the early 1990s. Henley's, the bus builder and car dealership group, eventually sold that 1960s coachbuilding business to Mike Bush, and it was relocated to Basingstoke. Eden then joined Bob Jankel, the car designer and builder of the Panther range. Together, they built the Tempest and an ocean-going schooner. But the timing for a luxury-goods initiative was bad at the tail end of the Gulf War. Eden went to work for the Land Rover dealer, Follett.

One day, Eden tracked down the owner of Radford, the daddy of all the Mini coachbuilders, and offered the owner some money for the name. The original owner had been running it as Radford Racing—a connotation that had no real bearing on the history of the brand. Eden moved the Radford name into a ready-made workshop, based near Luton in Bedfordshire, in June 2005.

The unexpected e-mail he received from Monaco was from a car collector and, the facts suggest, a wealthy man. His story was a rare one. This collector had two Radford Minis that had been built as a pair. They were both De Villes, but the distinctive feature was that they had both been stretched by 12 inches. One had a growly fast Cooper engine. That was kept at the English home in Windsor. The other was a town car—a 1-litre, left-hand-drive automatic kept in the toy town of Monaco. The owner had no further use for the UK long-wheelbase Cooper. It was sitting in a sad little heap and had been for a year. Would Radford buy it back?

Eden was pleased to. His new company was pressing on, happily making Radford conversions of new MINI. But it would be no hardship to have one of the past glories in

front chairs are from either a Rover 200 or Sterling and are leather trimmed. The horsepower increase from the Cooper engine makes it very noisy. Replacement of the plastic dash with an aluminium panel helped, as did sound-deadening of the doors. Sound-deadening was fitted in the grooves of the floorpan with an additional layer of material over the top.

The new door trims with wood capping had to be built out a little to allow space in the hollow for the electric window winders and central locking gear. All the door panels were carpet and leather, and the floor mats were all hand-stitched with leather edging. The engines were built by John Cooper's own workshop, had twin carbs, and knocked out 120 horsepower—a lot for those days but only half the output of the quickest 1.6-litre BMW MINIs.

The Coming of the Mini Limos

Harold Radford was the gentleman tailor of car conversions. He was an archetypical English gent who rode to hounds in the winter and played tennis at country homes in the summer while the hounds were on the beach. He went to Cambridge, of course, but the family shipping business bored him, so he borrowed money from his father and opened a car dealership in 1936.

Three years later, the war put an end to all that normal stuff, and Radford became a spymaster of sorts. It was expected of Cambridge boys. Spies required nondescript vehicles to transport them from job to job, and Radford provided, modified, and equipped them. He was also required

the company showcase, and this unique car would have been that all right—£30,000 ($56,537.70 U.S.) in 1993 money when it was built. The deal was done and the car transported from Windsor to the factory.

All of the stretch is in the doors, and the extra space is conferred on the front legroom. That meant that the roof, floor, door frames, doors, and door trims had to be remade. It had a very early Mini air-conditioning unit borrowed from the factory-fitted, Japanese-spec, original-equipment list.

The fascia was completely retrimmed and fitted with Radford-branded Smiths dials. The leather headlining comes down to waist level. The rear seat is a split-fold. The

Radford today with full air dam (left) and breather.

to provide transport for parachutists. They needed to get to various airfields in haste and needed to be well rested when they got there. His transporters were converted from American wagons and offered six sleeping berths and huge stowage for the chutes and equipment.

Thus, the war effort provided Radford with his apprenticeship as a carriagemaker. After the war, his training as a gentleman led him to Rolls and Bentley as suppliers of root stock to which he grafted luxurious wooden station wagon bodies. They were popular—a dozen were sold.

Distinctive wheels and oval exhausts.

In 1957, the Radford Motor Show exhibit at Earls Court in London was a Bentley Countryman with a pull-out picnic table in the rear that doubled as a grandstand and had a warm-water washbasin and an espresso machine fitted in the rear. Gentlemen's motorcars were getting luxurious.

Then Radford's father died, and Harold had to fulfill the promise he had made to manage the family's shipping business. The coachbuilder was sold to John Kary and Chris Mclaren, but Harold stayed with it as a consultant and travelled widely on behalf of his successors.

It's much harder with modern MINI to mess with the dash.

By 1963, Radford was ready to exploit the Mini's potential and exhibited three versions of the Mini de Ville—the full-on model at £1080 ($2,035.36 U.S.), the slightly less luxurious Bel Air, and the basic De Luxe. The names and concept ran seven years to 1970.

Journalist Tony Hogg wrote an observant piece about Radford for the November 1965 edition of *Road & Track*. His opening observation was: "One of the most surprising aspects of the American automotive world is the almost complete lack of facilities to enable the wealthy man to spend any real money on his car. America is by far the wealthiest country in the world [not any more, chum] but if you spend eight grand on a limousine from Cadillac, Ford, Mercury, or a Lehman-Peterson Lincoln, you have got the most the industry can offer. Fortunately, the Europeans take better care of their millionaires . . . . "

Hogg reviewed the Radford Mini and the marvels of its electric window lifts and twin-speaker radio and concluded that it was quite easy to spend $5,000. "The $5,000 Mini would seem to be something that almost anyone could do without. However, it has strong appeal to people who normally drive a Rolls or a Bentley but need something more nimble for city streets and are not willing to make any sacrifices as far as comfort and performance are concerned."

The thing in the workshop that tickled Hogg most on the day of his visit was a bus chassis that was being modified to provide separate quarters for the hired help, a passenger seat that elevated hydraulically clear through the

The seats are the most obvious enhancement.

roof for taking movies, and a hydraulic tailgate at the back to swing a Mini aboard like a dinghy. The beast was known as the Transcontinental Carabus.

Then, as now, Radford customers were described as very wealthy and, although not particularly concerned about the size of the bill, they "get hopping mad if they can detect any fault in the workmanship."

Under Hogg's nose during his visit, a secret car was being prepared for a secret customer—the famous Radford Mini bought by Peter Sellers for Britt Ekland. In 1967, Mike Nesmith of the Monkees had one. So did all four of the Beatles.

Harold used to know how to mix it with the tasty ladies of the 1960s. In the attic of his home at Conford, Near Liphook, Hants, after the death of his widow in October 2005, the current owner found a photograph of Harold with the actress, Gina Lollobrigida sitting on his knee. The current owner contacted Eden and offered him a number of souvenirs from that attic clearout, including Radford's framed certificate of membership of the The Institute of British Carriage & Automobile Manufacturers, dated November 1965.

Chapter 9

Get Involved: A Guide to Learning More and Seeing Other Dimensions of the Mini Tradition

The great joy of the Internet is that you can keep up-to-date with MINI business and interact with the newsmakers and gatherers. There are a number of sites that recognize the enthusiasm for MINI and have made that car the centrepiece of their coverage.

MINI2.com is a British site that styles itself as the leading independent MINI-focused website and carries a large and efficiently managed archive of the press release picture from the last five years of MINI. Paul Mullett, who runs, it obligingly recommends MINI2.info as a good German forum, newminiclub.nl for the Dutchmen, and clubmini.com.au for the boys and girls in Oz. NorthAmericaMotoring.com covers consumer interest on MINI in a similar way, but from an American perspective.

A U.S. forum that shares MINI ownership experiences is BMW-Mini-Cooper@yahoogroups.com. It is essentially interested in things that happen: "Anyone else heard this noise? Can you get a decent run-flat tyre? How do you deal with the heavy, wide-opening doors? Can you drive long distance without tiring?"

Minilist.org is a UK ring devoted to classic Mini in the UK. Members of the webring share help on acquisition and restoration and spend a great deal of time arranging meets and club activities. Insularity, enormous pride in the classic car, and some hostility to the new are pretty evident. The group started in a slightly different form 12 years ago. "There are about 700 people in touch throughout the UK," says John Bullas, the ringmaster. It's like being able to go to hundreds of old garages for advice.

If you don't like to ask, you can go look. Believe it or not, there is an Internet Mini encyclopaedia at IME.org.uk with over 200 pages, which is, as Bullas puts it, "reaching a conclusion." In other words, those people who have an expertise or opinion have contributed, and there is not much in the way of new talent coming through to swell the sum of knowledge.

One of the little tricks that become clear after a short period of contact with the group is that the spare parts traders are not all dyslexic. The fact that they have to advertise as "official Minny spare parts" and such is because BMW

Russ Swift—the fastest MINI driver on two wheels.

MINI Challenges run all over the world. This was a shot of the close racing from the 2005 World Final.

Opposite Page: New MINIs in the remake of *The Italian Job*—rated one of the best on-screen car chases of all time.

is quite rigorous about building its fresh and trendy new image and does not want dilution from the classic crew trading on its copyright brand name. BMW is quick to take legal action over breaches. Bit stuffy; not like the relaxed attitude of Rover, is the way that Minilist folk summarise.

Gabe Bridger runs the most laid-back MINI website. He gave it a general motoring title, but it's hooked on MINI and so far has not broadened the editorial more than a smidge. Bridger has a virtual presence called MotoringFile.com that has been going for three years in a comfortable, trend setting manner. He tells everyone what the new MINI will be like long before BMW has told its own dealers or the press. Beneath him, in his secret organisation, is a team of nameless agents who break commercial confidentiality (possibly) and submit tittle-tattle to Bridger.

Bridger is an amateur in that he has a day job, but he is a creative director by trade and has a feel for the way that a new website should develop. It seems as if the audience—and there are about 10,000 people watching on a daily basis—likes his approach.

Classics and modern get together at MINI United 2005.

The whole point of the site is the feeling of community. Bridger writes in weblog format. So do a few of his pals. Then the 500-or-so people out there, who like to talk back as well as watch, react with ideas of their own. All of it is about the product. The hot topic is what the next new MINI should be like.

Just recently, the naming of the imminent wagon version of the MINI came up. R55 (the code name) has been exhibited at motor shows four times, and 2008 has been given as the launch date for this new derivative. In classic Mini days, the estate car styled itself Traveller or Countryman, but in the collapse of the BMW-Rover relationship, either someone forgot to renew the rights to those names or BMW does not deem them suitable in the new age. Whatever applies, it is clear that there is no obvious name choice, and something better is being sought.

MotoringFile.com gets on the case. The subject was introduced to an attentive audience. Within minutes, the answers came back from all corners of the globe. It was a brainstorm that BMW might have lavished many Euros upon in a meeting or a superheated think-tank. Instead, all BMW had to do was to read MotoringFile.com, and it got 150 ideas popping up in fewer minutes, plus the destruction of the bad ideas and the reasoning behind the rejections. Brits, Americans, and Germans are to the fore. Australians are well involved. So are the Italians.

They don't come much more reduced. The Speedster is the handiwork of Gavin Wakeley. *Michael Whitestone*

MINI without losing touch with the heritage of the classic Mini.

There was Frank, toiling away at his new desk at Ferrari (and then subsequently toiling away at the parent company, Fiat), trying to keep the world racing car champion ahead of the game in road cars (and then trying to keep Fiat out of the hands of the auctioneers) when suddenly he popped up with an e-mail congratulation for MotoringFile.com. "He was good," says Bridger. "He is a supporter." This is how reputations are born in the new communications age.

Some of the more interesting contributions have unknown sources. "The way of the internet is that people can just leave messages under pseudonyms," says Bridger. "Are they BMW people? They might be. It's hard to know. I suspect some of them are. Certainly the contributors from the U.S., Germany, and the UK seem the best informed."

"It was one of those days where you realise what a powerful tool the Internet is," Bridger says. It was not the first such moment. The first occasion that he sat bolt upright while moderating the feedback e-mails after work was when he suddenly came across the name of Frank Stephenson, the laddie who sketched the shape of the new

It is pretty obvious that there is a guiding hand from the MINI mavericks in the shadows somewhere. It is in the

You don't have to be big to be a ground burner. Steve Moor's custom favourite is all flame and false teeth. Model aircraft canopies make the fake over-riders. The side frame has been chopped by 6 inches. *Alisdair Cusick*

interests of the brand to keep focus, intrigue, and controversy stoked up. But it is all subtly done. No one asks, and no one says. It is all down to Bridger, as moderator, who selects what shows on the site and what does not, to make sure that he is not spoofed or set up.

It is interesting how people of a similar type can be drawn to one another by admiration for, or affinity with, a particular car. Bridger drives a MINI. His is an all-black Cooper S. "I am a car enthusiast, and I really enjoy driving it. It is small and nimble. I like the design. I am drawn to the aesthetics. We have nothing else like it in the States. Although it is quick, it is not terrible on petrol. Certain attributes are important. Some of us like not to be wasteful."

Mini in the Movies

For those who can't get enough of MINI, there is a chance to see the car as a film star. In his book, *The Greatest Movie Car Chases of All Time*, Jesse Crosse rated *The Italian Job* at number four and *The Bourne Identity* at six. Both have police chases. Both have some hair-raising cityscape Mini driving sequences that make full use of the car's small scale.

Number four all-time great car chase: *The Italian Job* in 1969 starred Michael Caine in the lead role. He was himself already a Mini owner and enthusiast. His character, the villain Charlie Croker, plans an audacious scheme, bankrolled by the urbane crime boss Mr. Bridger, played by Noel Coward. The cunning plan is that if Turin is gridlocked after the heist, the police will not be able to pursue the getaway cars. The gold bullion is nicked, the traffic is disrupted, and the three Minis—laden with gold—rush down steps, across roofs, and through the sewers of the city. Finally, they run up a trailed ramp into the rear of a converted coach as it is driven along the autostrada. Remy Julienne, one of the most famous of all stunt drivers, was stage manager for the driving sequences and destroyed 16 Coopers in the process. It's breathless stuff and captures the spirit of Mini motoring perfectly.

Number six all-time great car chase: Cut to 2002, Paris and *The Bourne Identity*. By now, a Mini is more familiarly known as a battered old wreck, and this one is owned by the girlfriend of the man on the run from the CIA—there always is one. Hero Jason Bourne (Matt Damon) does battle with the famously anarchic Parisian traffic to evade his pursuers. The chase is through alleyways and down steps, across pavements, and the wrong way up one-way streets. Jason demonstrates a mean command of wheelmanship, and all the emphasis of the theatre is won from the exchanged glances between Jason and the car's owner, the lovely Maria. The police motorcyclists are closing in but don't spot the Peugeot 405 pulling out from the side turning. Cue massive impact, tortured metal, and the usual hiss of escaping air, water, and villain.

Helen Webster sits and thinks. Behind her waits many more months of dirty work. *Martin Vincent*

Opposite Page: It looks like a film set, but this is the way home from the dealer U.S.-style. Ken Russell bought from Albuquerque, then clocked up 3,006 delivery miles getting home. His homespun MINI adventure story is at www.sparerib.net/mini with many more.

The Classic Car Has Its Own Monthly

Rebuilding classic Minis is something that blokes do on their own or with a mate. They take too long, spend too much, and get verbally flayed by their partners for scrubbing the cylinder head in the kitchen sink. Right?

Not exactly.

There's Helen Webster to neatly provide the counterpoint. She is the editor of *Mini Magazine*—a magazine that you might have thought was a bit of a lad's mag in a diminutive sort of a way. It's turned out from the fabulous old Roman town of Bath in the southern English countryside.

Webster is not just a trained observer and chronicler. As any reader of her monthly magazine will know, she is a full-on, fully involved, dirty-finger-nailed, signed-up stripper and rebuilder. There's many an English petrolhead who would swap you all his original workshop manuals, a pair of period Recaros, and three pints of lager for such a find.

Ken Russell calls in to the Phoenix MINI Club meet with his newly collected car.

the winter of 2005, rented an unlit, unheated barn and set about fettling a wreck.

As is the tradition in these matters, it was unclear to the buyer's naked eye just how much of a wreck the Mini 25 was—though the asking price of £150 ($282.69 U.S.) did not promise very much. When she came to fit a new door, it became clear. The Mini had been in an accident at some stage in its youth, and one side was shorter than the other. The new door was never going to fit. That was just one of a long list of impossible problems that had to be resolved by editor and boyfriend Gavin as they learned their way around the restoration puzzle.

Every bit that went in it was original, and when Webster got to the interior trim and realised it would be very difficult to recover the Metro Turbo seats and everything else cheaply from commercial companies, she just borrowed a sewing machine, bought two rolls of the original vinyl, and set to. The greatest find was a period boot-lid-mounted reversing light. Final value of the car? About £3000 ($5,653.77 U.S.). Would she ever engage in such folly a second time?

"Well, I've just bought my next project—a 1964 Wolseley Hornet," Webster says. "It cost me three hundred

Ms. Webster was born into it all. Her dad bought a yellow Mini Clubman as celebration the day that his daughter was born and drove up to the hospital with his head out of the driver's window, waving a bunch of flowers. Neil Webster is still at it and keeps a small stable of Minis, including a Sport Pack and a Mk. II Cooper S replica.

The Mini affliction affected Webster's life to such a degree that she met boyfriend Gavin at a Mini show and, in

The 1977 van is a hot rod hero wherever it goes. It flipped into a field in 2002 but was back in its current fettle later that year. *Alisdair Cusick*

Steve Moor is a member of the Band of Gypsies Mini Owners' Group. He first spotted his chop donor when he worked for Simply Minis. *Alisdair Cusick*

fifty pounds, and I'm just about to start welding a new front end on . . . ."

Why does Mini attract the petrol-heads and the clubbable in a way that other cars do not? "It's still loved and enjoyed because of its character. You can do a lot with it. You can personalise it by painting it pink and fitting the furry dice and it does not look silly!"

Webster is a great guide to what goes on in the UK Mini scene because she reports on it and makes the news month by month. "There is a big Mini concours scene supported by people who want to show one another their personal touches, or the quality of their restoration, or the big refurbishment. And they want to win prizes that recognize the quality of what they have done. The British Mini Club is a major organiser that does two outdoor events, a track day, and an indoor show at Bingley Hall in Stafford. There are a handful of people who travel from

Mini magazine and a succession of British concours judges have routinely described this as the best standard Mini in the country. *Gerard Hughes*

Chris Kryzewiec has even ensured that all the original badges are refitted and that the text is legible. *Gerard Hughes*

Right: The buck stops—and the job starts—here. *Martin Vincent*

place to place with stunningly beautiful cars that have so much of themselves in them that the cars are trailered to events. But in the main, it's just the ordinary Joe who has stripped a car back to the original spec and then makes full use of it."

Webster's is a working-class car (and now a prize-winning working-class car at that) because she uses it every day to get to work, but others will prefer to get the perfect leather interior and exact right nuts and bolts and then keep the car in a garage. When it comes to concours prizes for original conditionthings can get a tad heated.

The man to beat at the original condition game is Chris Krzywiec, whose Cooper holds the Autoglym car of the year award for originality.

First timer's fettling. Webster's restoration is a prizewinner. *Martin Vincent*

Carlo Rally winning cars, which—hopefully—will never escape from captivity but will always be around for inspection and a reminder of those four, heady 1960s years of competition in the snowy mountains above Monaco. Racers split their time between circuits, and hillclimbs, and grass tracking, while rally drivers prefer forest track.

The most recent trend is to see just how far the original Mini concept will stretch, both in terms of the adaptability of the body and the performance available from whatever sort of engine can be made to fit. Stuart White, for example, was last heard of trying to midmount a brace of R1 motorcycle engines into the car, while Stuart Meads thought that an RS engine might be the way to go. The bright approach would be to choose a Mini Clubman, which has the taller and longer engine bay, into which to fit the muscular stuff. But there is plenty of admiration available for tackling the harder job and using the round-nose Mini as a starting point.

There are purists who prefer to revisit tuning of the original A-Series power units. These guys will use current

Other guys like to modify, customise, or just race, and there are plenty of ways to do all of that. There are also cars that need to be left exactly the way they are. How cross would the cognoscenti be if anyone dared to break that rule? For example, Mini registration number 621 AOK, which is in the Heritage Motor Centre in Gaydon in the English Midlands, is the oldest production Mini surviving—the sixth off the production line in 1959. Then there are the Monte

Pickup (left) and saloon from the front. *Gerard Hughes*

Peter White made the pickup. Ade Middleton made the saloon. *Gerard Hughes*

Right: From the rear, all is clear. There is a 1-litre Yamaha bike engine in each of these. *Gerard Hughes*

knowledge and modern methods but start with the old power mill rather than heaving it out and relying on something modern and fearsome. Retro tuning, they call it. You live with the classic appearance, including the original 10-inch wheels if need be, but get everything you can out of the engine. Each to his own. All approaches have their admirers.

Once the shell of the car is considered fair game for corruption, anything goes—lower roofs, fabricated panels, and even a custom-made steel body reminiscent of Lamborghini's style, as in the case of Kelly Davison's purple parody.

But because so many of the 5 million Minis made still remain, it's hard to generate real value from either rarity or

Above: Of course, the car is properly accessorised with genuine Quant goodies. *Martin Vincent*

Left: Ruth Lowe has a thing about Mary Quant and has the best limited-edition Quant car. *Martin Vincent*

restoration. The bigger money is in the Mk. 1 Cooper S and the last Rover Mini with the Sport Pack, which fell in value to as low as £1,000 ($1,884.59 U.S.). It is now back up to £6,000 ($11,307.50 U.S.) at best, making some of the buyers who hung on for appreciation very happy. The limited editions, though, have not been as good at holding value.

Webster's Mini 25, for example, was never going to make her rich, and she knew it. Webster actually is a bit of a bandit in that she does not really give a stuff about rigid originality. After caring deeply about originality where it mattered, she has fitted a Mk. 1 Mini Cooper badge on the bonnet just "because I like it!"

Some do care completely, though. Ruth Lowe has made a hobby out of collecting Mary Quant merchandise to adorn her 1989 Designer limited-edition Mini and has become quite a cult figure at shows because of it.

Epic Journeys

Then there are the epic journeys for recreation. *The Italian Job* journey is the big daddy of them all and is run every year for children's charities by Freddie St. George. Dozens of people in all types of Minis drive from London to Turin in a gaggle, attracting interest and bemused photographers wherever they go. The 1969 film, *The Italian Job*, is a crime caper starring Michael Caine as a bullion thief.

"We are 100 strong now and take our Minis every year to Turin to try and retrace the steps of the cult film," says

Gavin Wakeley's thigh-high Mini Speedster was a three-year labour of love. The road-legal racer runs the standing quarter-mile in 13.7 seconds from an over-bored 1,399cc Metro Turbo engine.
Michael Whitestone

Freddie. "We don't drive down the steps of the church though. During the original film, the directors just winged it—did the stunt without getting local permission and apologised later."

It's an epic that has some of the older and less well-prepped cars gasping for breath, but the esprit de corps ensures that everyone makes it there and back. That's the thing about Mini clubs—because the car itself generates so much affection, a general sense of goodwill swirls around all who get involved.

Stunt Driver Displays

You have to wonder why Russ Swift isn't a motorcyclist. You also have to wonder if his is a stage name. Russ spends his

Kelly Davison's special is wide enough for a brace of headlamps on each side. *Martin Vincent*

Below: The highly original side treatment looks like providing the chance to bolt on a set of wings. *Martin Vincent*

whole time motoring on two wheels. And when he parks, he parks in the gap between cars that no other vehicle could fit into. Yet all of this is done in a MINI. Because he is a stunt driver. And yes, that is his real name.

Swift's work started soon after he became recognised as a bit of a special talent. He won the BTRDA and RAC Autotest Championships in 1982 and 1983 in a Mini Cooper S and a Moke. He turned to show work, and his first displays were in the autotest Cooper S in which Paul, his son, also won the BTRDA and RAC Autotest Championships in 2005 and 2006. Paul is just as swift.

After using a chopped-down Mini for auto testing, Swift converted 45 Minis to convertibles for road use. This was the basis for the Austin Rover convertible model. He ran a display team for Austin Rover from then until its demise.

Many of his shows were in Minis, including the anniversaries—Mini 30, 35, and 40—at Silverstone, where he used an arctic truck to recreate the coach scene from the original *The Italian Job.*

"In 1999, I set a Guinness world record for parallel parking in two seconds in a space thirty-three centimetres longer than the Mini. That's just over a foot." It sounds impossible, but the proof is on the web. Just Google Russ Swift and see the impossible preserved on video.

Swift performed at the launch of the MINI to dealers in Manchester in 2001 and continuously operated a display team for them after that. Highlights included the British Motor Shows at NEC, Mini Adventure Live, and MINI Open Air Theatre. He also performed at the North American launch at the New York Motor Show and at premieres of *The Italian Job* film in New York, Amsterdam, and Leicester Square, London. The MINI used for most displays is an absolutely standard MINI Cooper S convertible. A second MINI Cooper has only one modification—a locked differential. This is the car driven on two wheels. Swift gets a maximum of 3 miles from a set of tyres.

He now holds three Guinness world records—parallel parking in the tightest space, J-turn in the tightest space, and the fastest doughnuts.

Phil Herring's Mini, based on a Clubman front and with an unforgettable paint scheme. *Alisdair Cusick*

Chapter 10
The Men from the MINIstry in Munich

Opposite: The American market for MINI is as strong as the demand in the UK.

In one tiny corner of the rolling industrial acres that are home to BMW in Munich, there is an area branded MINI. It looks little different from the rest from outside, but on the inside everything changes. Most important of the changes is the mindset. MINI arose from thinking differently in a structured way. MINI will only pursue its adventure if the wild-child personality is maintained.

To secure an exploration of MINI Munich for this book, there had to be a promise that interviewees would not be identified. There are no public faces for MINI below the main board. There are only members of a team, and that's the way they like it, because that is the way that they feel things work best.

So what follows is a puree of the thoughts of five people, all of whom are very much on the same wavelength when it comes to talking about future development. Their strength of purpose is tangible, and their thread of the rational is taut and reassuring.

The five reveal that the pattern for MINI is Porsche. If you thought the pattern must be VW Beetle, don't sneer; listen up. The rationale is this: the Porsche 911 concept—four years younger than Mini, in that its first appearance was 1963—is so good that it does not change other than to modernise, to adopt newly available technology, and to meet changes in environmental and safety legislation. It's compromised—the cabin could be better, the golf clubs won't lock away, and the luggage needs sending on ahead. But it has a loyal band of admirers and a growing pool of aspirants. So leave it alone.

Imagine if classic Mini had not been squeezed by shrinking budgets within BL and Rover and that it had been evolved on a regular basis, and you can convince yourself that it would have developed organically into the car that MINI is today in just the same way that the Porsche 911 has.

Beetle, on the other hand, is a nasty aberration. The engine is at the wrong end. The seating position is for van drivers. The driving experience is just plain wrong. As a result, the opinion-formers who decide what is cool and what is not have pretty much abandoned it. It has become a car that the girls buy because they like the shape. That spells

Left-hand drive already predominates for MINI.

death by a thousand phrases of faint praise in the male-dominated car magazines.

The other thing MINI delivers that aligns it with the pattern of Porsche is the driver pleasure. It has all been carefully thought through and nothing is missing. Ride and handling are reminiscent of the classic car. The engineering team fought tooth and nail to ensure that the steering part of the handling package was right and had to incur the extra cost of electric/hydraulic rather than electric steering.

"The steering feel of the car was indirect and artificial. It was very hard to convince some of our colleagues that the go kart feel we deemed essential was not being achieved. We got some of our race drivers together at Gaydon [the test track], and they said that in its present state, they would never drive the car. That did the trick."

The aural pleasures are all there. The Cooper S JCW in particular was tuned for the drive-by music. There is a great deal of marketing value in an exhaust note that turns heads on the pavement and earns a nod of approval. That is not something that BMW would own up to, is it? Deliberately causing noise in the inner city is very non-mainstream brand, but for the boys in the MINI T-shirts in the corner of BMW's Munich site, it was kinda okay. It suits the rebel streak and has edge to it that helps the brand image.

One of the marketing people gives the analogy of Red Bull. Truck drivers drink Red Bull and were always expected to. But if the initial advertising had been aimed at them, the market might have remained limited to the kings of the road.

Badged as a Mini Cooper S, ACV30 took the three winning 1960s cars on a parade lap before the start of the 1997 Monte Carlo Rally.

Instead, the product was aimed at the youth market. It became cool to be seen with a Red Bull in hand, and suddenly Red Bull was a cool product, aspiring, and okay across the social divides. So it is with MINI.

Another analogy that almost works for the men of Munich is the Mazda MX5, though the construction of the story is somewhat different, because Mazda has not relied upon one of its own historic products, but someone else's. The basic, great-handling, two-seater sports car is a spiritual descendant of the Lotus Elan, and it has the great virtue of purity of purpose. It retains basic simplicity in order to achieve minimal dimension and great poise and balance, but is in no sense a muscle car within its class in the way that Cooper S and 911 Turbo are.

There had been three finalists in the internal design competition to get at the heart of future MINI. Other than Stephenson's winning design, there was the Spiritual, which was the rational, logical approach to refreshing Mini from MG Rover and which would have taken BMW down the Mercedes A-Class route without adding too much to the market. There was also the ACV 30, a Cooper sports car that would have competed in the Audi TT/Mazda MX5 arena. Crucially, though, it might have cannibalised sales from the BMW Z Series.

The proponents of a contemporary Mini replica insisted on preserving the upright A-pillars and screen and the flat roof, which together were terrible for aerodynamics and fuel

From the side, ACV30 is a very clear missing link between classic Mini and current MINI.

consumption. It is also a wasteful design in that the wheelhouse is inboard of the waistline.

"You never do that. You never waste space by deliberately making the cabin narrower than the overall width of the car. Rolls-Royce does it, but it has plenty of width to waste."

A cost disadvantage that the design team faced from the outset was that there was a brief to sell in all markets of the world—something that no other small-car maker does—not even Polo, which is absent from the U.S. market. That guiding principle makes the car extremely expensive to design, because it has to meet so many varied crash test requirements.

MINImal Management

The product boys liked the short decision process that Segler got working from on high. MINI development was a virtual board of three guys with marketing, engineering, and production all hanging together. There was a board meeting without fail every week. Nothing was more important than that meeting. And decisions got made. When reports were needed to the main BMW board, the guys would turn up in bright orange MINI T-shirts and kept on keeping on in building a discrete identity separate from the BMW formality.

The front profile sets ACV30 apart. Skinny motorcycle mud-guards and a near-pillarless roof give it a very individual look.

"For a long while, we were the bad guys. We were rule breakers. We were causing discomfort within the organisation. Our drive to be extrovert and chic—to live the brand that we were trying to build—was difficult for BMW. Now, everyone wants to be a part of MINI."

The funding for MINI was an issue with the Rover brand costing so much time and money and causing such a problem. In the end, the money to continue the process was smuggled out to the men in orange T-shirts in a rather unconventional manner by Joachim Milberg (who was the BMW Group chairman from February 1999 to May 2002) in defiance of Bernd Pischetsrieder, BMW chief executive up to that time, who had started to withhold funds in 1998.

The summer of 1999 was the moment that MINI found its public voice, though it was still something of a whisper. During the Silverstone race circuit 40th anniversary party for Mini, the German gang showed a film of the Cooper company and then a fleeting set of images of the new MINI that was by then under wraps and was set for production at Longbridge. A quick on-site response survey suggested that 70 percent of the Mini buffs there liked the confection that was due in the market 18 months later. The other 30 percent apparently did not dislike the car so much as disliking the fact that the endeavour was being run by a German gang.

Raw paint and full harness emphasise the Mini sporting lineage.

The eventual unveiling of new MINI was punctuated by an outbreak of bumper stickers from the creative side of the classic Mini clubs. There was even a dedicated website: IHateTheBMWMini.org. Some of the more acceptable slogans were:

"You don't have to have a big one to be happy."

"Made in England; contains no artificial BMW additives."

"Dear BMW, There is only one Mini, one *Italian Job*, and one legend; so go home. The End."

These days, there is rather more elbow room for the new MINI amongst the classic Minis at the annual shows and meetings. Indeed, many of the leading tuners have started to bring their performance and customising bins to the shows with a pretty full set of offerings for the new beast. Even the IHateTheBMWMini.com boys have withdrawn hostilities to ensure that they have some continuing commercial viability. The spat has reached its natural end—another confession, no matter how reluctant, that BMW has nourished the brand and done well.

Meanwhile, the MINI men in Munich were very keen to ensure that the traditional BMW relationships with performance enhancers did not spread across to MINI. The most persistent would-be infiltrator was Alpina, long the preferred BMW partner on serious performance equipment. Mike

Cooper's operation on the south coast of England enjoyed an even warmer embrace from that moment on to ensure that the BMW hierarchy did not lose sight of the Cooper heritage's importance to the marketing programme. Mike Theaker, the engine guru who has had a huge influence in the Cooper tuning kit business, became even busier.

The cold war between the old enemies was not entirely one-sided. The Brits were not blameless in creating ill feelings. BMW wanted to make sure that classic Mini was not soiling the nest in the final couple of years of its existence, and selling it was becoming an embarrassment. The English management was invited to make a few basic improvements. "English journalists all accepted that Mini had no ABS and no airbags. What was harder to deal with was the fact that the steering wheel was not straight and that one corner of the bonnet was higher than the chrome grille."

The German team wanted a better carpet fit and better engine bushes. The wheel spats were by then being fitted by drilling screws straight through into the galvanised metal and breaking the rustproof seal. "We asked the Longbridge management why there were no predrilled holes in the body, and we got the answer that they could never get them to line up.

"The management told us that they had been making Minis for forty years and they needed instruction from no one. If we wanted to go into the plant, we had to ask permission in advance and then permission again on the day from the union and the duty foreman. If we went in without permission, there was always trouble."

Pointers to the Future

With new MINI just about clear of the development team's care and into full production, attention can turn to the next initiative. The MINI Traveller—or whatever it might be called in its final form—will be the first new derivative since the convertible. There have been four international showings of concept cars that tickled the taste buds a little. But first, there has to be some engineering of the convertible for it to come off the new platform. For a year or so, while that work is going on, the convertible will remain as is. There is engineering work to be done on diesel also. The selection of the Toyota diesel was a choice that made itself in 2001 in that it was the only block that would fit in the MINI engine bay. Now, after the engineering changes, there is a wider choice, and there is space for the diesel to carry a turbo and to have the engine mounted transversely either west-east or east-west. The new unit may be from Peugeot, the petrol-engine partner, or MINI might remain with Toyota. The gang admits that there have been advantages in a business relationship with a Japanese maker—not something that happens every day of the week within BMW. A choice of diesel units is needed—especially a performance version with turbo—to help further with the brand's average fuel economy.

Once diesel and convertible modifications are out of the way, all eyes will be on the yet-to-be-named Traveller/Clubman/Estate/Shooting Brake/Countryman.

Chapter 11
What's Next?

The MINI managers love a tease. The "we do things differently" (different from BMW that is) mantra is taken to a whole new level when it comes to dribbling information through internet chat rooms and enthusiast clubs, anonymously correcting misinformation, and stimulating the reaction that helps design a new car.

New MINI is upon us, and initially it will be a three-door saloon only. The convertible will continue on the old platform for a while. Once the engineering resources are available, a soft-top will be redesigned to come off the new platform.

There is a Traveller to come. That's promised and scheduled for 2008. Ever-evolving variations of the concept vehicle have been appearing across the world at Frankfurt, Tokyo, Detroit, Geneva, and London motor shows. What was effectively an estate car (or "Touring" in BMW-speak) was first built as the Morris Mini Traveller and the Austin Countryman and then morphed into the Clubman Estate. There was always a minivan alongside the passenger vehicle. The historic figures show that Traveller production ran at somewhere between 10 and 20 percent of the equivalent saloons. It was in production from 1960 to 1982. The overall length was up by 10 inches on the saloons, while wheelbase was 4 inches longer. Initially, there was a woody framework that mimicked the estate version of the Morris Minor but was stuck on and had no structural benefit whatsoever—a fact that was proven subsequently by offering the all-metal version with a discount of a mere £19 ($35.81 U.S.).

The Traveller was confirmed for production at Detroit on January 10, 2006, and the promise then was that it would be in the shops "within three years." It would be a bit of a surprise if it was much later than the end of 2008. The engineers do not have a massive amount of other things to do now that the new platform is done and in production, and there has been a year's worth of Traveller styling prototypes. The name is proving to be sticky because MINI is insistent on uniformity across markets, and Traveller, Countryman, and Clubman are either not available or not appropriate in all 70 national markets.

It is clear that the role of Traveller will be part fashion and part function. The stretch in the platform length will allow a full four seats as well as, or instead of, more luggage space. There is a supposition that there could be both a

Smart white wheels and party-time canopy.

Tail up and ready for roddin'.

Smart attempt at a crew cab on a six-wheeler pickup.

Lowered, stretched, and dammed.

Birthday cake atop the 20th anniversary model heads the parade.

Mike gets them mounted up for an effortless drive home.

four-door and a five-door (or possibly six-door) and that the rear side doors could be front-opening suicide doors in the style of the Mazda sports coupe. Maybe there will be just one rear side door. Many of the lobbyists among would-be purchasers want four-wheel drive, which makes a lot of sense. It's hard to see any of those concept cars making much progress into the Alps, down to the beach, or along the Monte Carlo Rally special stages without it.

The styling cue from the original Traveller is the double-opening tailgate doors, though the original adoption of double doors was simply because the assembly line at Longbridge was not wide enough to accommodate a single rear door swinging open.

One Shape, Many Forms
The MINI Concept Geneva focuses on accessibility and convenience. Front and cargo doors both work on parallelogram kinetics, so that they can swing clear of the door aperture and open beyond 90 degrees. The rear has a fitted cargo box with a lid that folds up for a transparent partition, and the lid slides out to make loading easier. Additional storage is created in the rear side window apertures and can be accessed

from inside and out. The presentation of Concept Geneva was as a rally support vehicle, so the vehicle needs speed and comfort for the crew on the road for several days without rest and plenty of clever hidey holes for the bits and pieces. Front seats swing around for access to the rear load, and the rear seats fold flat for extra luggage area. The spare wheel goes up the roof and forms a power bulge, which adds to the muscular look deriving from the flared wheel arches.

MINI Concept Detroit is based on a winter sports theme designed in the colours of the U.S. flag. The roof rack and boot have convenient fixings for carrying snowboards, skis, and mountain bikes. The stowage bins are filled with goggles and gloves.

The MINI Tokyo project was a rather neat picnic car with a knife and fork set mounted where the rally car maintenance kit would be for the Geneva Concept.

There have been hints that a MINI sports car could be in the cards, and it has to be said that a two-seater must be a consideration, given that MINI powertrains are all so lusty. But the lack of success of many other diminutive sports cars, such as the smart roadster, suggests that volumes could be minimal. Care would also be needed to avoid a clash with small BMW-branded two-seaters and a compact sports car interior would not lend itself to the MINI's signature exotic interiors.

The first sports car concept predated the on-sale date of new MINI by three years. The ACV 30 (Anniversary Concept Vehicle, 30 years on from Mini's last of three Monte Carlo Rally wins) was developed when BMW and Rover were still buddies. It led a parade of Monte-winning Minis at the 1997 Monte Carlo Rally. It turned out to be pretty sympathetic to the look of the saloon car built at Oxford three years later. It used the MGF running gear, the Rover 1.8-litre 16-valve K-series engine, and aluminium body panels.

An even funkier teaser was the MINI Canyon Carver. It was designed by the BMW Group design studio in the United States and shown at the Los Angeles Car Show. It was described as the ultimate L.A. machine. It had a high power-to-weight ratio and an open deck at the rear for surfboards, snowboards, hang-gliders, and the like. MINI designers are keen on the idea that they should offer special-purpose derivatives. There is some very joined-up thinking about the potential to make statements with your MINI. A man arrives at the beach in a Porsche 911, and everyone looks at him and says, "Okay, rich, discerning, tasteful; maybe a bit of a poser." The guy arrives at the beach with a MINI Carver with a full set of his-and-hers surf kites of the best possible taste, and the thinking is, "Coooool." Function and fashion together in perfect harmony is the new cool. Now go and work it out with a production car offer. The proposition suits MINI, in that it is pushing ahead faster and faster with the online build-your-own-car offer, now extended to the 2007 MINI with interior trim textile and colour changes. If anyone can get special-purpose cars off a dedicated assembly line, MINI can.

The Past as a Guide to the Future

If the past can be any guide to the future, Hildebrand and the

Four up in a Moke. Not quite the job for the weather.

There's always an oily sponsor looking for visibility.

boys will have been thumbing through the history of classic Mini, looking for clues. There is no richer history of adaptation, modification, and enhancement spawned by front-drive and subframe construction.

BMW has itself entered into the right spirit with auto show concept cars and the excellent XXL project, which gave us a MINI stretch limo with a luxurious central cabin for two aft of the concealed chauffeur and a rear hot tub. It has to be the best way to deal with a motorway hold-up on the way to Cornwall for the summer holiday.

There was a 12-seater stretch in classic Mini days—20 feet in length and a great showroom draw but never a road-going tease in the way that MINI has become.

A van comes off a Traveller quite easily of course. A pickup body was part of the classic Mini commercial range. The Carver is essentially an updated Mini Pick-Up and if there is any intention to produce such a thing, then the United States is the place to originate the design philosophy.

The Mini Moke was first designed for the army. Issigonis himself was keen that it should become the basic

Above: Here's a happy camper . . . and a great pattern for BMW's forthcoming MINI Traveller.

Left Top: An aero-screened three-wheeler leans in.

Left Bottom: Union Jack roofs and six-wheel pickups are familiar, but *together*!?

Half Mini, half punt.

Top Right: A horror story from the usually well-respected Tickford.

Bottom Right: A Mini Safari six-wheeler with canvas tilt, built by Stimson.

You can get a Mercedes radiator and lamps on a Mini. Would BMW approve?

With another powerplant in the boot, it becomes a Twini and highly dangerous.

utility vehicle of choice, to be dropped by parachute with the forward troops. There were many specialist derivatives of this stripped and basic vehicle, ranging from beach buggies to open-sided hotel courtesy cars.

By far the nicest of the sports cars was the Landar, very much a specialist vehicle built between 1963 and 1972 only, and a winner of the Sports Car Club of America under-1,300cc class.

Above: A 20-foot 12-seater Mini with roof bars that gave their name to saloon bars.

Top Right: William Towns—designer of the wedgie Aston Martin Lagonda—thought that you could make an even shorter four-seater Mini. He was right.

Bottom Right: Mr. Plod the Policeman with the latest in crime deterrence—and a curly-wurly flex on his mobile phone. Very now.

Above: Broadspeed found a fastback formula for the Mini.

Top Right: Leyland Cars engineers provided the assurance that Minis can swim at a raft race in 1977.

Bottom Right: The photo from the Longbridge exhibition hall shows the idea for hotel courtesy cars.

A Mini Moke can be launched into orbit, but only tail first.

Top Left: The owner claimed that if one engine was not running too sweetly, he would swap ends and U-turn.

Bottom Left:
Issigonis only went so far with his abbreviation. A two-seater Mini almost fits in the palm of your hand.

The gorgeous little Can-Am replica was called the Landar and won races.

Right Top: The Stimson Minibug was a first-rate contributor to the dune buggy era.

Right Bottom: Mercedes lamps did become the hot must-have for a while.

There is, of course, a MINI car available for kids. Either that, or small steering wheels have fallen out of fashion.

Left Top: This was the original marketing artwork for the new Mini Pickup.

Left Bottom: This may have been the original Minibus, but more likely it was a double-decker for routes with low bridges.

BMW intends sand-casting 10-foot plastic beach buckets.

Right: There is room for four passengers in the MINI XXL, so long as the backward pair sits very still.

There may be some issue with cresting the rise in a multi-storey car park.

Top Right: So that's what lurks in the trunk. Water and rose petals are standard.

Bottom Right: XXL it may be, but it still has a pert little bum.

The MINI Carver study never made it further than the desktop, but it remains food for thought.

Right: The L.A. paper design for the Carver concept contained a wide range of permutations for a MINI activity vehicle.

Mini Canyon Carver

The Mini Canyon Carver concept incorporates open-air fun, as well as a driving experience normally reserved for less practical sports cars. The rear compartment can become a storage bed for surfboards, snowboards and other outdoor gear; when not in use, it is easily converted back to a normal four passenger seating arrangement. With over 200 horsepower, and a lightweight carbon fiber structure, the Canyon Carver is equally at home on mountain roads, city streets, or at the beach.

Chapter 12
What's New?

Over the summer of 2006, BMW had several bites at releasing the details of the new MINI and generated a good head of steam. First, there was a call in July from the press office to certain of the leading lights in motoring journalism to get across to the racing circuit at Zandvoort in Holland, where they would find MINI development engineers in the final stages of testing the new car. Some secrecy was maintained. Some of the new external styling details of the car were masked with tape, and the whole of the dashboard was covered with fabric to obscure it. Journalists were given every encouragement to thrash the thing within an inch of its life round the circuit and then tackle wet and dry handling courses. Some hired-in cameramen stood by to take commissions from the journalists. Some details of the car's new features were disclosed in writing. Some were winkled out of the development engineers led by Detlev Welters, the director of product management for MINI, who thought it great to be extemporizing rather than developing cars for the day.

Some of the long lead magazines, such as Britain's *What Car?*—which did some comparative shots for this book to allow

study of the style changes—were lent photographic cars for private studio work within a couple of weeks. Then, in August, came a press release for all and sundry with just five official press release pictures. There was due to be an official launch of new MINI at the Paris Auto Show in September/October. The on-sale date was to be November 18, and there was to have been a torrent of fresh info at that time to remind small-car consumers worldwide that the premium product in the sector was fresh, better, faster, cleaner, and even more frugal.

Most of the journalists who went to Zandvoort came away with the same impression. The MINI Cooper S (the only variant available) was less of a beast. While the average user would undoubtedly enjoy the quieter behaviour and softer ride, there was some regret amongst the diehards that the mechanical racket, gearbox whine, and snap-in, snap-out steering characteristics had gone. Many who have lived with similar characteristics in classic Mini will also mourn the loss of those particular traits. Possibly.

When Hilton Holloway of *Autocar* magazine took the new MINI round Zandvoort, he came away with this impression:

Thanks to the consistency of detail shots taken by the monthly British What Car? *magazine, it is easy to highlight the changes to new MINI.*

"The Cooper S demonstrates much greater civility than the outgoing car. The ride is very compliant and, at low speeds, the electrically assisted steering is beautifully weighted. You may complain that the steering lacks real feel, but it is much lighter at the rim. Sporting drivers might lament the loss of effort required, but the MINI can be positioned with fingertip ease, and it's quick enough with just 2.7 turns, lock to lock. The comfort of the new S is also a surprise. Thanks to redesigned front suspension and taller towers, the new car has an extra 8 mm of travel. That, together with the lighter engine, transforms the front end ride."

There is more bonnet between grille head and air scoop on the new car.

This is a quick car, without doubt, but the smoothness of the engine's response and the turbo's near-seamless integration make driving the new Cooper S less of an event than in the old model. Although the old supercharged version wheezed and rattled a bit, it felt alive. The new Cooper S is more refined and very quick, but it lacks the visceral thrills of the old car.

Life for motoring writers is somewhat different to owners. Writers like to have easily definable distinguishing

characteristics. MINI purists and motorsport enthusiasts might hanker for that a little also. But, in the main, what the folk want is what they get—a comfortable car with lots of performance on tap. The outgoing Cooper S is still available on the used car market and may well become a treasured classic for its make-me-hurtle demeanour. It is a very difficult car to drive slowly. Its aural pleasures invite you to drive like a hooligan. But the new car is better, and the U.S. market will take to it even better than they have already.

BMW folk were frightened to death when they presented the second-generation MINI to the waiting world, even though they knew that they had done very well with the first one. They knew that they had to spend quite a bit of money making all

The new boot is deeper, thanks to the barreling of the boot panel, and will hold an extra 10 litres.

the crash test changes for the successor. They knew that noise, vibration, and harshness could be improved. What they did not know was whether or not the audience would be satisfied with the delivery of so little apparent change so soon after the 2001 launch of the first-generation MINI.

When confronted by a journalist at the full press launch in October in the sunny Spanish city of Barcelona, with a summary that second-generation MINI was "very clever," designer Hildebrand was immediately attentive and curious: "Do you think so?"

The funky centre console pillars have gone, and the door panel inners are simpler.

It *was* clever to consolidate success by maintaining the look and then adding the technical bits that made the difference, because there is plenty of opportunity to make major visual changes later on. The Traveller (actual name as yet undetermined) will have every opportunity to be fun, funky, and different, and the derivatives after that will discover how far the natural MINI buyers want to depart from the mainstream MINI concept, and how much they will experiment. That will condition the next derivative, and so on. Expect something radical about every three years.

One thing that the crew worries about is the degree to which MINI needs to be of English origin to succeed. At the moment, it assumes a huge importance, but there will come a time when BMW will have to decide whether or not to maintain its corporate philosophy and ensure that production follows the market. A Plant Oxford expansion has taken capacity up 20 percent to 240,000 cars a year, but if growth continues to climb at the present rate, it will be up against the ceiling again with no way of climbing farther.

Although the buildings would be full, there is spare land on site—enough to push production capacity to 350,000 with a new factory. However, once new factories come up for approval, there will be an immediate call to site

Switches have moved to the steering wheel so that centre dash clutter is removed. Note the neat MINI emblem switch arrangement.

them in the strongest area of demand. That means the United States, logically, where there is already a market of nearly 40,000 cars a year. Taking costs in strong British pounds and selling cars for weak U.S. dollars has never been good commercial sense and has crucified Jaguar's business. The United States becomes highly desirable as a production site.

Segler and the boys would probably risk that if the brand could stand separation from its English origin, and the chances are that by the time the decision needs to be made, the brand will have an identity of its own that transcends nationality.

MINI marketing people believe that they may have inadvertently tapped into a new sort of consumer; postmodern, they call him. This consumer is not driven by the mob but finds what he likes by himself. The "build your own car" facility already caters for that to a degree. MINI suits the 3–5 percent of society that does not follow the crowd but rather leads change. They see MINI not just as a premium brand, but as a rebel brand also. Marketing thought then takes the MINI phenomena up a level with MINI brand as a destination, with product offers from other consumer segments that have all the same standards of design, performance, and entertainment. In Barcelona, there was a tentative display of mini Smeg refrigerators with reduced MINI roof decals on the convex fridge doors. We get the idea.

The filler cap alone can distinguish new from old.

It's all very interesting, exciting . . . and distracting for the tight group of people whose job it is to plan the future. One of the more senior think-tank members said, "I can't release all my dreams, even to myself. I get so excited."

If it all goes to plan, the new MINI revolution will be a repeat of the classic Mini revolution, which, in its day, created a massive aftermarket for accessories and performance bits and a parallel fashion industry epitomised by the miniskirt. Except that BMW will do its best to sell all the extra bits *before* the car is assembled.

So what do the consumer champions think about second-generation MINI now that it has been subjected to the full test on the mountainous public roads of Spain? It's pretty uniform really—an excitement for the competence of the small car tempered by a slight disappointment that the wild child has gone to be replaced by a mature adolescent. Tim Pollard, in *What Car?* Magazine, asked rhetorically: So would you still want one?

"You bet. Like its predecessor, the new MINI is the very essence of cool. Which other £11,000 ($20,735.00 U.S.) supermini is sought by image-conscious trendsetters from estate agents to rock stars, including Madonna? (She has a black one in London to go with the black Range Rover and paid full price; MINI has never placed cars with celebs.)

"The new turbocharger engine is less charismatic than the engine in today's car; however, the supercharger whine and wallop are replaced by quieter power delivery. It's

The front bonnet line no longer splits the radiator grille. The indicators are now in the main lamp cluster.

quicker but less dramatic," Pollard adds.

Richard Bremner is another road-test scribe who knows his stuff, and he did a long appraisal of second-generation MINI for *Autocar*: "You'll hear decidedly more cultured sounds from beyond the firewall, the Getrag's six-speed linkages have been fettled, and the more polished actions of the controls suggest a MINI that has grown up a little."

He goes on: "Gone are the excitable whinings of the blower to be replaced by a smooth-rising four-pot hum that's enlivened by a deepish resonance, if you are bold with the throttle, that makes this engine fleetingly sound like a big-bore version of the original Mini's A-Series engine. You can also get treated to the odd pop and blat from the twin-pipe exhaust. This engine is not as rawly exciting as the old super-charged lump."

That is why it was so much loved by the MINI Challenge racing community. Not only was the Tritec making the right sound when the flag dropped, but it was unburstable even under the most arduous circumstance of boiled-off cool and seeped-out oil.

MINI 2 could have been made more of a screamer with a much higher rev limit than 6,500cc, but BMW funked it. The engineers were under instructions to get more sophistication onto the car to keep onside with the American market's priority for comfort over performance. Also, high

In the period when the market was taking stock of the new car and taking delivery of the old, the Cooper S Works GP was arriving with the 2,000 people allowed to order it. It has an impossibly long name, quite out of keeping with the MINI's duty toward brevity, and in its full-out style must be known as the BMW MINI Cooper S John Cooper Works Grand Prix. Even as an acronym—BMW MCS JCW GP—it consumes more than a quarter of the alphabet and takes longer to say than to accelerate to 60 miles per hour. The limited-edition GP was built in Italy by the design house Bertone to overcome the capacity shortage at Plant Oxford.

There is an inglorious link between Bertone and MINI, in that the Italian company was the contractor that created the unlovely Innocenti Mini hatchback. British Leyland decided to buy Innocenti in 1972 and put a financial controller, Geoffrey Robinson—subsequently a ruinous managing director of Jaguar—in charge. Having set the wheels in motion, Robinson returned to the UK. De Tomaso bought Innocenti in 1975 and continued production of the original Mini and the Bertone version, which sat on a shortened platform and was to all intents and purposes a two-seater hatchback. It survived until 1992, when Fiat bought Innocenti.

MINI GP was stripped to achieve a weight loss of 35 kilograms—most of that achieved by tossing out the back seat and fitting a transverse stiffening bar across the rear cabin instead. There is also a lightweight aluminium rear suspension setup that has found its way into the second-generation MINI to aid its quest for better fuel economy. The supercharger on the Brazilian 1,600cc develops 214 horsepower at 7,100 rpm and 184 lb-ft of torque at 4,600 rpm, leading to a 0–60-mile-per-hour figure of 6.4 seconds. Top speed is 149 miles per hour.

There is bodywork aplenty: skirts, a front air dam, and an in-your-face spoiler at the back. The downforce is so great that, together with upgraded 16-inch brake discs, the car gets squirmy and wriggly under heavy braking; it's safe and fun but not efficient.

The glasshouse is shallower, there is much cleaner detailing on the apron, and the rear lights are very different.

revs would have required stiffer valve springs, and that would have lowered the fuel economy. MINI was not exactly struggling to get an improvement from the new engine. It has achieved a 25 percent improvement to 41 miles per gallon on the combined cycle with a commensurate drop in the CO_2 emission level, which gives a better corporate tax level.

The cabin feels classier and neater, though still familiar. The large, round central speedometer is the eye-catching feature of the interior. It's that big because it is more than a speedo. Minor gauges are in there too, and it accommodates

infotainment and sat-nav as well. The rev counter is still on the steering column, and the curvy strengthener/armrest/door-pull arrangement is still sculptured as an ornament in the inner door casing. The aluminium pedals are in a wider footwell that now accommodates at least two size-13 boots, either side. A brand-new feature that will not get too much coverage until journalists start road-testing in the dark is the ambient lighting that dusts the colour in five stages between blue and orange. The idea is that you feel cooler on a hot day with blue light and warmer on a cold day with orange, and it works as a mood enhancer. Expect the same from other makers.

MINI is not a small car in the way that it used to be, but it is still compromised in terms of being able to accommodate

The seat catch has changed for easier access to the rear. Rear armrest arrangement has also changed.

four adults in comfort. Three can do it if the third is prepared to contort into the rear seat. MINI is a foot shorter than comparable hotshots, such as the Renault Clio 197, and 6 inches shorter than a comparable premium car in the small-car sector, such as the A-Class Mercedes. But really it has to be judged as a car for two people that completely lacks the capacity to take your mates to the races. Child seats are fine.

BMW is quite surprised how many young people can afford a premium-priced car in the sector and who can overlook the fact that they need a second car for the four-some or family outing. The four-seat market is something that the forthcoming stretched MINI (shall we guess it will be called Clubman?) will be able to address.

There can be no doubt now that the MINI revival is here to stay. In the United States, there has been a sudden recognition that diminutive is not just socially responsible; it can be both comfortable and rewarding as well. It is 50 years since Issigonis was told to create a small car, and his brainchild, in its new guise, is quite capable of being refined for another 50. Ever aware of the valuable legacy that it has inherited, BMW chose November 18 as the launch date for the second generation of new MINI. Had he lived so long, Issigonis would have been 100.

Above & top right: New wheels for the new car on the right. No surprise there.

Opposite Left (Top & Bottom): The side repeater décor no longer gives access to mini bugs.

Opposite Right (Top & Bottom): The rear apron now kicks up over the two side-by-side barrels.

Bottom Right: How it all ends. Head for the far-distant horizon.

Appendices

Mini Chronology

1956
August: Issigonis was commissioned to design a small car in haste. AD015 (Austin Drawing Office 15) was conceived

1959
August: Austin Seven (Se7en) and Morris Mini Minor were launched. Named Austin 850 and Morris 850 for United States and France

1960
January: Van introduced with 848cc engine

1961
January: Mini Pickup introduced

October: Riley Elf and Wolseley Hornet introduced with traditional radiators and lengthened boots

1962
Austin Mini Cooper and Morris Mini Cooper launched with a 998cc engine

Austin Seven name dropped

1963
Mini Cooper S introduced with a 1071cc engine and larger disc brakes

1964
Mini Moke introduced with fabric roof

Base Cooper 998-cc engine becomes a shortened-stroke 997cc

A 1275cc Cooper engine and a small 970cc were developed specifically for racing

Hydrolastic suspension introduced to supplement the rubber cone system

Mini wins the Monte Carlo Rally for the first time

1965
Automatic gearbox introduced
The 970cc engine was discontinued

Mini wins again at Monte Carlo

1966
Mini wins at Monte Carlo but is disqualified on a headlamp technicality

1967
Introduction of the Mark II body type

Mini 1000 super deluxe saloon and estate introduced with 998cc engine

Mini completes the hat trick of Monte Carlo victories

1968
BMC merges with British Leyland to form BLMC under Lord Stokes

Moke discontinued

1969
Austin and Morris names both dropped from the badging of Mini.

April: Mini 1000 introduced with winding windows and concealed door hinges
Production of 998cc variant ends

October: Mini Clubman saloon introduced

Clubman estate replaces Coutryman Traveller

Mark III body variant of the 1275cc Cooper S introduced

Mini Cooper saloon discontinued; replaced by 1275GT

Mini stars in *The Italian Job*

Elf and Hornet discontinued

1970
Mini Clubman introduced

1971
The Innocenti Mini Cooper 1300 began production in Italy and the Authi Mini Cooper 1300 in Spain

Mini Cooper S discontinued

Peak production year: 318,475 cars built

1972
Cooper phased out by British Leyland

John Cooper's company takes back the name and sells Cooper kits for Minis sold in Japan

1975
BLMC fails and is nationalised

1977
Sir Michael Edwardes succeeds Lord Stokes as head of British Leyland

1979
Honda takes a stake in BL

1980
Mini Clubman discontinued

1982
Feb: Estate, van, and pickup all discontinued

1988
BL "denationalized" by sale to British Aerospace

1990
Mini Cooper name reintroduced by the factory

1991
June: Mini Cabriolet introduced

July: Cooper reintroduced with MG Metro 1275 engine

1992
May: New 1.3-litre engine

1994
BMW buys Rover

2000
October: Longbridge and Rover is sold to Phoenix

Last classic Mini produced; a total of 5.3 million had
been made

Investment for production of the new MINI at Longbridge is stopped

December: John Cooper dies

2001
BMW builds new MINI at newly modernised Cowley plant near Oxford

The Spec of the Hot One
MINI Cooper S John Cooper Works GP

Body

No. of doors/seats	3/2
Length/width/height (unladen)	3,655/1,688/1,416 mm
Wheelbase	2,467 mm
Track, front/rear	1,446/1,452 mm
Turning circle	10.66 M
Tank capacity	50 approx. ltr
Cooling system including heater	6.0 ltr
Engine oil	4.8 ltr
Transmission fluid incl axle drive	Lifetime
Weight, unladen, to DIN/EU standard[1]	1,120/1,195 kg
Max load to DIN standard	280 kg
Max permissible weight to DIN standard	1,400 kg
Max permissible axle load, front/rear	890/730 kg
Max trailer load[2]	NA
Braked (12%)/unbraked	–/– kg
Max roof load/max towbar download	75/– kg
Luggage compartment capacity to DIN standard	670 ltr
Air resistance	0.35 x 1.98 C_D x A

Power Unit

Configuration/No. of cyls/valves	Inline/4/4
Engine management	Siemens EMS 2000
Capacity	1,598 cc
Bore/stroke	77/85.8 mm
Compression ratio	8.3:1
Fuel grade	91–98 RON

MINI GP continued

Max output (at 7,100 rpm)	160/218 kW/hp
Max torque (at 4,600 rpm)	250/184 Nm/lb-ft
Electrical SystemBattery/installation	55/rear Ah/–
Alternator	105/1,470 A/W

Chassis and Suspension

Suspension, front: Single-joint Mc Pherson spring strut axle with anti-dive

Suspension, rear: Longitudinal arms with centrally pivoted track control arms, z-axle

Brakes, front: 16-inch John Cooper Works disc brakes, vented
    Diameter: 294 x 22 mm

Brakes, rear: Discs
    Diameter: 259 x 10 mm

Driving stability systems: Hydraulic twin-circuit brake system with ABS anti-lock brakes, EBD Electronic Brake Force Distribution and CBC Cornering Brake Control, ASC + T Traction Assistance and limited-slip differential. Optional DSC Dynamic Stability Control at no extra cost. John Cooper Works sports brakes with 16" disc brakes acting mechanically on rear wheel

Steering: Electrohydraulic steering (EHPAS); 2.5 turns from lock-to-lock

Steering ratio, overall: 13.18: 1

Type of gearbox: Six-speed manual
    Gear ratios

I	**1) 4.455**: 1	
II	**1) 2.714**: 1	
III	**2) 1.333**: 1	
IV	**2) 1.089**: 1	
V	**1) 1.333**: 1	
VI	**1) 1.089**: 1	
R	**2) 2.818**: 1	

Final drive **1) 2.87/2) 4.24**: 1

Tyres: 205/40 R18 82W RSC

Rims: 7J x 18"alu

Performance[3]
Power-to-weight ratio to DIN standard: 7.0 kg/kW
    Output per litre: 100.1/136.1 kW/bhp

Acceleration	0–100 km/h	6.5 sec
	Standing-start km	– sec
In 4th/5th/6th gear	80–120 km/h	5.3/6.6/8.8 sec
Top speed		240 km/h

Fuel consumption in EU cycle

Urban 11.8 ltr/100 km	
Extra-urban	6.8 ltr/100 km
Composite	8.6 ltr/100 km
CO_2	207 g/km

Miscellaneous

Emission standard	EU 4
Ground clearance	– mm

[1] Weight of car in road trim (DIN) plus 75 kg for driver and luggage.
[2] May be increased under certain conditions.
[3] Performance and fuel consumption figures relate to RON 95.

MINI One and MINI One CVT

Body

	MINI One	MINI One CVT
No. of doors/seats	3/4	3/4
Length/width/height (unloaded)	3635/1688/1416 mm	3635/1688 /1416 mm
Wheelbase	2467 mm	2467 mm
Track, front/rear	1458/1466 mm	1458/1466 mm
Turning circle	10.66 m	10.66 m
Fuel tank capacity	50 ca. l	50 ca. l
Cooling system incl. heater	5.3 l	5.3 l
Engine oil	4.5 l	4.5 l
Unladen weight according to DIN/EU	1065 / 1140 kg	1080 / 1155 kg
Max. load (DIN)	430 kg	430 kg
Max. permissible weight (DIN)	1495 kg	1510 kg
Max. permissible axe load, front/rear	870/730 kg	870/730 kg
Max. trailer load[2]		
Braked (12 %)/unbraked	650/500 kg	650/500 kg
Max roof load/max towbar download	75/- kg	75/- kg
Luggage comp. capacity VDA	150 l	150 l
Drag coefficient/front area	0.35 x1.97 c_X x A	0.35 x 1.97 c_X x A

Engine

	MINI One	MINI One CVT
Layout/No. of cylinders/Valves	Inline/4/4	Inline/4/4
Engine management	Siemens EMS 2000	Siemens EMS 2000
Displacement, effective	1598 cm^3	1598 cm^3
Bore/stroke	77/85.8 mm	77/85.8 mm
Compression ratio	10.6:1	10.6:1
Fuel grade	91–98 RON ROZ	91–98 RON ROZ
Max. output	66/90 kW/bhp	66/90 kW/bhp
at engine speed	5500 rpm	5500 rpm
Max. torque	140 Nm	140 Nm
at engine speed	3000 rpm	3000 rpm

Electrics

	MINI One	MINI One CVT
Battery/location	46/front Ah/–	46/front Ah/–
Alternator	90/1280 A/W	90/1280 A/W

Chassis/power transmission	MINI One	MINI One CVT
Front suspension	Single joint MacPherson spring strut axle with anti-dive	Single joint MacPherson spring strut axle with anti-dive
Rear suspension	Longitudinal struts with centrally pivoted control arms, Z axle	Longitudinal struts with centrally pivoted control arms, Z axle
Brake, front	Ventilated disc brake	Ventilated disc brake
Diameter	276x22 mm	276x22 mm
Brake, rear	Disc brake	Disc brake
Diameter	259x10 mm	259x10 mm
Driving stability system	ABS, CBC, EBD	ABS, CBC, EBD
Steering	EHPAS, 2.5t turns from lock to lock	EHPAS, 2.5t turns from lock to lock
Overall ratio:1	13.18	13.18
Type of transmission	5speed Getrag –Manual	CVT(automatic)
Transmission ratio		
I	13.755:1	Variable
II	7.954:1	Variable
III	5.231:1	Variable
IV	3.921:1	Variable
V	3.351:1	Variable
R	13.434:1	3.82:1
Final drive ratio	No separate ratio	5.76:1
Tyres	175/65R15 84T	175/65R15 84T
Wheels	5.5Jx15´´ Steel	5.5Jx15´´ Steel

Performance

		MINI One	MINI One CVT
Power to weight ratio (DIN)		16.1 kg/kW	16.4 kg/kW
Output per litre		41.3 kW/l	41.3 kW/l
Acceleration	0–62 mph	10.9 s	12.7 s
in 4th/5th gear	50–75 mph	11.9 s	14.9 s –
Top speed		112 mph	106 mph

Fuel consumption[3]
(EU cycle)

Urban	29.4 mpg (imperial)	25.9 mpg (imperial)
Extra urban	54.3 mpg	47.9 mpg
Combined	41.5 mpg	36.7 mpg
CO_2	164 g/km	187 g/km

Miscellaneous

Emission classification	EU3	EU3
Ground clearance	139 mm	139 mm
Insurance group	5E	5E

MINI Cooper and MINI Cooper CVT

Body	MINI Cooper	MINI Cooper CVT
No. of doors/seats	3/4	3/4
Length/width/height (unloaded)	3635/1688/1408 mm	36/1688 /1408 mm
Wheelbase	2467 mm	2467 mm
Track, front/rear	1458/1466 mm	1458/1466 mm
Turning circle	10.66 m	10.66 m
Fuel tank capacity	50 ca. l	50 ca. l
Cooling system incl. heater	5.3 l	5.3 l
Engine oil	4.5 l	4.5 l
Weight,unladen, according to DIN/EU	1075/1150 kg	1090/1165 kg
Max. load (DIN)	430 kg	430 kg
Max. permissible weight (DIN)	1505 kg	1520 kg
Max. permissible axle load, front/rear	870/730 kg	870/730 kg
Max. trailer load[2]		
Braked (12%)/unbraked	650/500 kg	650/500 kg
Max roof load/max towbar download	75/- kg	75/- kg
Luggage comp. capacity VDA	150–670 l	150–670 l
Drag coefficient/front area	0.35x1.97 c_X x A	0.35x1.97 c_X x A

Engine		
Layout/No. of cylinders/Valves	Inline/4/4	Inline/4/4
Engine management	Siemens EMS 2000	Siemens EMS 2000

	MINI Cooper (cont'd)	MINI Cooper CVT (cont'd)
Displacement, effective	1598 cm^3	1598 cm^3
Bore/stroke	77/85.8 mm	77/85.8 mm
Compression ratio	10.6:1	10.6:1
Fuel grade	91–98 RON ROZ	91–98 RON ROZ
Max. output	85/115 kW/bhp	85/115 kW/bhp
at engine speed	6000 rpm	6000 rpm
Max. torque	150 Nm	150 Nm
at engine speed	4500 rpm	4500 rpm

Electrics

	MINI Cooper (cont'd)	MINI Cooper CVT (cont'd)
Battery/location	46/front Ah/–	46/front Ah/–
Alternator	90/1280 A/W	90/1280 A/W

Chassis/power transmission

	MINI Cooper (cont'd)	MINI Cooper CVT (cont'd)
Front suspension	Single-joint MacPherson spring strut axle with anti- dive	Single-joint MacPherson spring strut axle with anti- dive
Rear suspension	Longitudinal struts with centrally-pivoted control arms Z-axle	Longitudinal struts with centrally-pivoted control arms Z-axle
Brake, front	Ventilated disc brake	Ventilated disc brake
Diameter	276x22 mm	276x22 mm
Brake, rear	Disc brake	Disc brake
Diameter	259x10 mm	259x10 mm
Driving stability system	ABS, CBC, EBD	ABS, CBC, EBD
Steering	EHPAS, 2.5 turns	EHPAS, 2.5 turns
Overall ratio	13.188:1	13.188:1
Type of transmission	5-speed Getrag Manual	CVT automatic
Transmission ratio		
I	14.400:1	Variable
II	8.327:1	Variable
III	5.476:1	Variable
IV	4.105:1	Variable
V	3.509:1	Variable
R	14.065:1	3.82:1
Final drive ratio	No separate ratio	5.76:1
Tyres	175/65R15 84H	175/65R15 84H
Wheels	55Jx15" alloy	55Jx15" alloy

		MINI Cooper (cont'd)	MINI Cooper CVT (cont'd)

Performance

		MINI Cooper (cont'd)	MINI Cooper CVT (cont'd)
Power to weight ratio (DIN)		12.6 kg/kW	12.8 kg/kW
Output per litre		53.2 kW/l	53.2 kW/l
Acceleration			
	0–62 mph	9.1 s	10.4 s
in 4th/5th gear	50–75 mph	10.5 s	13.5 s –
Top speed		124 mph	115 mph

Fuel consumption⁰ (EU cycle)

	MINI Cooper (cont'd)	MINI Cooper CVT (cont'd)
Urban	29.1 mpg (imperial)	25.9 mpg (imperial)
Extra urban	53.3 mpg	47.9 mpg
Combined	40.9 mpg	36.7 mpg
CO_2	166 g/km	187 g/km

Miscellaneous

	MINI Cooper (cont'd)	MINI Cooper CVT (cont'd)
Emission classification	EU3	EU3
Insurance Group	8E	8E
Ground clearance	130 mm	130 mm

MINI Cooper S and MINI Cooper S Automatic

Body

	MINI Cooper S	MINI Cooper S Automatic
No. of doors/seats	3/4	3/4
Length/width/height (unloaded)	3655/1688/1416 mm	3655/1688/1416 mm
Wheelbase	2467 mm	2467 mm
Track, front/rear	1454/1460 mm	1454/1460 mm
Turning circle	10.66 m	10.66 m
Fuel tank capacity	50 ca. l	50 ca. l
Cooling system incl. heater	6.0 l	6.0 l
Engine oil	4.5 l	4.5 l
Weight,unladen according to DIN/EU*	1140/1215 kg	1160/1235 kg
Max. load (DIN)	430 kg	430 kg
Max. permissible weight (DIN)	1570 kg	1590 kg
Max. permissible axe load, front/rear	890/760 kg	890/760 kg
Max. trailer load²	not possible	not possible
Braked (12 %)/unbraked	not possible	not possible

Luggage comp. capacity VDA	150–670 l	150–670 l
Drag coefficient/front area	0.37x1.98 c_X x A	0.37x1.98 c_X x A

Engine

Layout/No. of cylinders/Valves	Inline/4/4	
Engine management	Siemens EMS 2000	Siemens EMS 2000
Displacement, effective	1598 cm?	1598 cm?
Bore/stroke	77/85.8 mm	77/85.8 mm
Compression ratio	8.3:1	8.3:1
Fuel grade	91–98 ROZ	91–98 ROZ
Max. output	125/170 kW/bhp	125/170 kW/bhp
at engine speed	6000 rpm	6000 rpm
Max. torque	220 Nm (lb-ft)	220 Nm (lb-ft)
at engine speed	4000 rpm	4000 rpm

Electrics

Battery/location	55/rear Ah/–	55/rear Ah/–
Alternator	105/1470 A/W	105/1470 A/W

Chassis/power transmission

Front suspension	Single joint MacPherson springs strut axle with anti-dive	Single joint MacPherson springs strut axle with anti-dive
Rear suspension	Longitudinal struts with centrally pivoted control arms, Z axle	Longitudinal struts with centrally pivoted control arms, Z axle
Brake, front	Ventilated disc brakes	Ventilated disc brakes
Diameter	276 x 22 mm	276 x 22 mm
Brake, rear	Disc brakes	Disc brakes
Diameter	259 x 10 mm	259 x 10 mm
Driving stability system	ABS, CBC, EBD, ASC + T	ABS, CBC, EBD, ASC + T
Steering	EHPAS, 2.5 turns lock to lock	EHPAS, 2.5 turns to lock
Overall ratio	13.18:1	13.18:1
Type of transmission	6-speed Manual	6-speed Automatic

Transmission ratio

I		12.789:1	4.044:1
II		7.793:1	2.371:1
III		5.651:1	1.556:1
IV		4.615:1	1.159:1
V		3.828:1	0.852:1
VI		3.126:1	0.672:1
R		11.944:1	3.193:1
Final drive ratio1.1		1:1	
Tyres		195/55 R16 87V RSC	195/55 R16 87V RSC
Wheels		6.5J x 16" alloy (runflat)	6.5J x 16" alloy (runflat)

Performance

Power to weight ratio (DIN)		9.1 kg/kW	9.3 kg/kW
Output per litre		78.2 kW/l	78.2 kW/l
Acceleration	0–62 mph	7.2 s	7.7 s
in 4th/5th gear	50–75 mph	6.1 s /7.7 s /10.5 s	-/- s
Top speed		138 mph	137 mph

Fuel consumption[3] (EU cycle)

Urban (imperial)		23.9 mpg	22.1 mpg
Extra urban		41.5 mpg	41.5 mpg
Combined		32.8 mpg	31.4 mpg
CO_2		207 g/km	216 g/km

Miscellaneous

Emission classification		EU3	EU4
Insurance group		15A	15A
Ground clearance		142 mm	142 mm

*Weight of car in road trim (DIN) plus 75Kg for driver and luggage

MINI One Convertible

Body

No. of doors/seats	2/4
Length/width/height (unloaded)	3635 / 1688 / 1415 mm
Wheelbase	2467 mm
Track, front/rear	1458 / 1466 mm
Turning circle	10.66 m
Fuel tank capacity	50 ltr
Cooling system incl. heater	5.3 l
Engine oil	4.5 l
Weight (DIN/EU1)	1165 / 1240 kg
Braked (12%)/unbraked	650 / 500 kg
Drag cx / A / cx x A	0.37 / 1.97 / 0.73 cX x A

Engine

Layout/No of cylinders/Valves	In line /4/ 4
Fuel management	Siemens EMS 2000
Displacement, effective	1598 cm?
Bore/stroke	77 / 85.8 mm
Compression ratio /Fuel type	10.6: 1 / 91-98 ROZ
Max. torque	140 Nm (lb-ft)
at engine speed	3000 rpm

Electrics

Battery/location	46 / bonnet Ah/–
Alternator	90 / 1260 A/W

Chassis/power transmission

	Brake, front
Diameter	276 mm (disc vented)
Brake, rear	
Diameter	259 mm (disc)
Driving stability system	
Steering	EHPAS
Overall ratio	13.18:1
Type of transmission	Getrag 252
Transmission ratio	
I	13.755:1

II	7.954:1
III	5.231:1
IV	3.921:1
V	3.351:1
R	13.434:1
Final drive ratio	1.00:1
Tyres	175 / 65 R15 84T
Rims	15-inch, steel

Performance

Power to weight ratio (DIN)	17.7 kg/kW
Output per litre	41.3 kW/l
Acceleration	0–62 mph
11.8 s	
in 4th/5th gear	50–75 mph
13.5 s / 16 s	
Top speed	109 mph

Fuel consumption[3]

(EU cycle)

Urban	28.2 mpg
Extra urban	49.6 mpg
Combined	39.2 mpg
CO_2	173 g/km

Miscellaneous

Emission classification	EU4
Insurance group	EU4
6E	

[1] Weight, unloaded, including 75 kg for driver.
[2] May increase under certain conditions.
[3] Information about performance and fuel consumption refer to ROZ 95.

MINI Cooper Convertible

Body

No. of doors/seats	2/4
Length/width/height (unloaded)	3635 / 1688 / 1415 mm
Wheelbase	2467 mm
Track, front/rear	1458 / 1466 mm
Turning circle	10.66 m
Fuel tank capacity	50 ltr
Cooling system incl. heaterl	5.3
Engine oil	4.5 l
Weight (DIN/EU1)	1175 / 1250 kg
Braked (12 %)/unbraked	650 / 500 kg
Drag cx / A / cx x A	0.37 / 1.97 / 0.73 cX x A

Engine

Layout/No. of cylinders/Valves	Inline /4/ 4
Fuel management	Siemens EMS 2000
Displacement, effective	1598 cm?
Bore/stroke	77 / 85.8 mm
Compression ratio /Fuel type	10.6 : 1 / 91-98 ROZ
Max. torque	150 Nm (lb-ft)
at engine speed	4500 rpm

Electrics

Battery/location	46 / bonnet Ah/–
Alternator	90 / 1260 A/W

Chassis/power transmission

Brake, front	
Diameter	276 mm (disc vented)
Brake, rear	
Diameter	259 mm (disc)
Driving stability system	
Steering	EHPAS
Overall ratio	13.18:1

Type of transmission

Type of transmission	Getrag 252
Transmission ratio	I
14.4:1	II
8.327:1	III
5.476:1	IV
4.105:1	V
3.509:1	R
14.065:1	
Final drive ratio	1.00:1
Tyres	175 / 65 R15 84T
Rims	15-inch, alloy

Performance

Power to weight ratio (DIN)	13.8 kg/kW
Output per litre	53.2 kW/l
Acceleration	0–62 mph
9.8 s	
in 4th/5th gear	50–75 mph
11.6 s / 14.4 s	
Top speed	
	120 mph

Fuel consumption[3]

(EU cycle)	
Urban	28.0 mpg
Extra urban	49.6 mpg
Combined	38.7 mpg
CO_2	175 g/km

Miscellaneous

Emission classification	EU4
Insurance group	9E

[1] Weight , unloaded, including 75 kg for driver.
[2] May increase under certain conditions.
[3] Information about performance and fuel consumption refer to ROZ 95.

MINI Cooper S Convertible

Body

No. of doors/seats	2/4
Length/width/height (unloaded) mm	3655 / 1688 / 1415
Wheelbase	2467 mm
Track, front/rear	1452 / 1460 mm
Turning circle	10.66 m
Fuel tank capacity	50 ltr
Cooling system incl. heater	5.3 l
Engine oil	4.5 l
Weight (DIN/EU1)	1240 kg / 1315 kg
Braked (12%)/unbraked kg	Not Possible
Drag cx / A / cx x A	0.37 / 1.97 / 0.73 cX x A

Engine

Layout/No. of cylinders/Valves	Inline / 4 / 4
Fuel management	Siemens EMS 2000
Displacement, effective	1598 cm?
Bore/stroke	77 / 85.8 mm
Compression ratio /Fuel type	8.3 :1 / 91-98 ROZ
Max. torque	220 Nm (lb-ft)
at engine speed	4000 rpm

Electrics

Battery/location	55 /boot Ah/–
Alternator	105 / 1470 A/W

Chassis/power transmission

Brake, front	
Diameter	276 mm (disc vented)
Brake, rear	
Diameter	259 mm (disc)
Driving stability system	
Steering	EHPAS
Overall ratio	13.18:1
Type of transmission	Getrag 285
Transmission ratio	

I	12.789:1
II	7.793:1
III	5.651:1
IV	4.615:1
V	3.828:1
V1	3.126:1
R	11.944:1
Final drive ratio	1.00:1
Tyres	195 / 55 R16 87V
Rims	16-inch, alloy

Performance

Power to weight ratio (DIN)	9.9 kg/kW
Output per litre	78.2 kW/l
Acceleration	0–62 mph
7.4 s	
in 4th/5th gear	50–75 mph
6. 6 s / 8.4 s	
Top speed	134 mph

Fuel consumption[3]

(EU cycle)	
Urban	23.9 mpg
Extra urban	39.8 mpg
Combined	32.1 mpg
CO2	211 g/km

Miscellaneous

Emission classification	EU4
Insurance group	16A

[1] Weight , unloaded, including 75 kg for driver.
[2] May increase under certain conditions.
[3] Information about performance and fuel consumption refer to ROZ 95.

MINI One D

Body

No. of doors/seats	3/4
Length/width/height (unladen)	3 626/ 1688/ 1416 mm
Wheelbase	2 467 mm
Track, front/rear	1458/ 1466 mm
Turning circle	10,66 m
Fuel tank capacity	50 approx. l
Cooling system including heater	5,3 l
Engine oil	4,3 l
Weight, unladen, to DIN/EU1	1115/ 1190 kg
Max. load to DIN	430 kg
Max. permissible weight to DIN	1545 kg
Max. permissible axle load, front/rear	870/ 760 kg
Max. permissible trailer load2	
Braked (12 %)/unbraked	650/ 500 kg
Max. roof load/max towbar download	75/ - kg
Luggage compartment to VDA	150-670 l
Air resistance	0,36 x 1,97 cX x A

Engine

Layout/No of cylinders/valves	Inline/ 4/ 2
Engine management	Bosch EDC 16
Capacity	1364 cc
Bore/stroke	73/ 81,5 mm
Compression ratio	17,9:1
Fuel grade	Diesel RON
Max. output	65/ 88 kW/PS
at engine speed	3800 rpm
Torque	190 Nm
at engine speed	1800–3000 rpm

Electrical system

Battery/location	70/ back Ah/–
Alternator	130/ 1820 A/W

Chassis and suspension

Front suspension	Single-joint Mc Pherson spring-strut suspension, anti-dive
Rear suspension	Longitudinal control arm with central traverse arms, Z-axle
Brakes, front	Disc brake vented
Diameter	276x22 mm
Brakes, rear	Disc brake
Diameter	259x10 mm
Driving stability systems	Hydraulic dual-circuit-braking system with antilock system (ABS), Electronic Brake Force Distribution (EBD) and Cornering Brake Control (CBC) as well as Automatic Stability Control + Traction (ASC + T). Optional Dynamic Stability Control (DSC). Mechanical hand brake acting on the rear wheels.
Steering	Electro-hydraulic steering (EHPAS); 2.5 tions from lock to lock
Overall steering transmission	13,18:1
Transmission	6-speed manual
Transmission ratio	
I	1) 4,583:1
II	1) 2,550:1
III	2) 1,114:1
IV	2) 0,878:1
V	1) 1,114:1
VI	1) 0,878:1
R	2) 2,833:1
Final drive ratio	1) 2,742:1
	2) 4,048:1
Tyres	175/65 R15 84T
Rims	5,5Jx15" steel

Performance

Power to weight ratio (DIN)	17,2 kg/kW
Output per litre	47,7 kW/l
Acceleration	0–62 mph
11,9 s	

33,9 s	0–1000 m	Overall	4,8 l/100 km
in 4/ 5th gear		CO2	129 g/km
10,1/ 11,7 s	50–75 mph		
Top speed		**Miscellaneous**	
	175 km/h	Emission classification	EU 4
Fuel consumption (EU cycle)		Ground clearance (unladen)	139 mm
In town	5,8 l/100 km		
Out of town	4,3 l/100 km		

MINI Cooper and MINI Cooper S. Specifications.
Model year 2007 (August 2006)

Vehicle	**MINI Cooper**	**MINI Cooper S**
Length	3699 mm	3714 mm
Width	1683 mm	1683 mm
Height (unladen)	1407 mm	1407 mm
Wheelbase	467 mm	2467 mm
Track front/rear	1459/1467 mm	1453/1461 mm
Weight, unladen, according to DIN/EU1	1065 /1140 kg	1130/1205 kg
Max permissible weight to DIN	1515 kg	1580 kg
Tyres	175/65 R 15 H	195 R 16 87 V RSC
Wheels	5,5J x 15	6,5J x 16
Engine		
No of cylinders/valves	4/4	4/4
Capacity	1598 cc	1598 cc
Output max	88/120 kW/hp	128/175 kW/hp
at	6000 rpm	5500 rpm
Torque max	160 Nm	240 Nm (260 with Overboost)
at	4250 rpm	1600–5000 rpm (1700–4500 with Overboost)

Performance

Top speed	126/203 mph/km/h	140/225 mph/km/h
Acceleration	0–62 mph	9,1 s 7,1 s
	0–1000 m	30,2 s 27,5 s
in 4th/5th/6th gear	50–75 mph	9,4 / 12.1 / 14.3 s 5,5 / 7.0 / 8.0 s

Consumption in the EU cycle

Urban	36.2/7,8 mpg/ltr/100km	31.7/8,9 mpg/ltr/100km
Extra-urban	61.4/4,6 mpg/ltr/100km	49.6/5,7 mpg/ltr/100km
Combined	48.7/5,8 mpg/ltr/100km	40.9/6,9 mpg/ltr/100km
CO2	139 g/km	164 g/km
Fuel	from 91 RON	from 91 RON
Emission category	EU 4	EU 4

[1] Weight of the car in road trim (DIN) plus 75 kg for driver and luggage.

Index

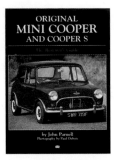
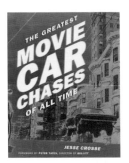

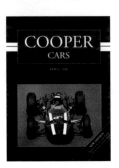
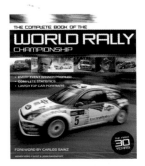
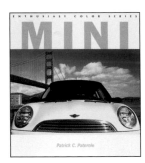